WORLD WAR II
HIROSHIMA & NAGASAKI

WORLD WAR II
HIROSHIMA & NAGASAKI

Published by Bookmart Ltd 2005

Blaby Road,
Wigson,
Leicester,
LE18 4SE
Books@bookmart.co.uk

Copyright ©2005 Taj Books Ltd

Copyright under International, Pan American, and Universal Copyright Conventions. All rights reserved. No
part of this book may be reproduced or transmitted in any form or by any means, electronic or mechanical,
including photocopying, recording, or by any information storage-and-retrieval system, without written
permission from the copyright holder. Brief passages (not to exceed 1,000 words) may be qouted for reviews.

All notations of errors or omissions (author inquiries, permissions) concerning the content of this book
should be addressed to TAJ Books 27, Ferndown Gardens, Cobham, Surrey, UK, KT11 2BH, info@tajbooks.com.

ISBN 1-84509-173-6

Printed in China.
1 2 3 4 5 08 07 06 05

Contents

To start his New Guinea campaign, MacArthur put on a cunning diversionary operation to make the Japanese believe they were going to be attacked frontally in the area of Wewak. Lieutenant-General Hatazo Adachi, C.-in-C. Japanese 18th Army in New Guinea, fell into the trap. April 22 was thus a day of easy triumph for the U.S. I Corps (Lieutenant-General Robert L. Eichelberger) which landed, without much difficulty, its 24th Division (Major-General F. A. Irving) at Tanahmerah Bay and its 41st (Major-General H. H. Fuller) at Hollandia and Aitape. When he had got over his surprise, Adachi tried to turn his forces round and re-establish his communications. During July the Aitape sector was the scene of furious fighting, throughout which Adachi urged on the Japanese 18th Army in terms of mingled despair and determination:

"I cannot find any means or method which will solve this situation strategically or tactically. Therefore, I intend to overcome this by relying on our Japanese Bushido. I am determined to destroy the enemy in Aitape by attacking him ruthlessly with the concentration of our entire force in that area. This will be our final opportunity to employ our entire strength to annihilate the enemy. Make the supreme sacrifice, display the spirit of the Imperial Army."

This appeal was understood and followed, but the time and trouble it cost Adachi to turn round gave the Allies an advantage which they did not let slip, especially as they were also able to decode the Japanese radio messages. And so, during the night of July 11–12, the 18th Army's counter-attack found the Allies alert and reinforced by Major-Generals Charles P. Hall's XI Corps and William H. Gill's 32nd Division. The Japanese were held.

MacArthur strikes along the coast

MacArthur was already hopping from one island to the next along the coast of New Guinea. On May 17, his 41st Division landed at Wakde, 125 miles west of Hollandia. On the 27th, a further hop of 200 miles brought him to Biak, where the Japanese put up fierce resistance. Virtually ignoring this as a local incident, he pushed on to the island of Numfoor on July 2 and on the 30th he reached the beak of the Vogelkop. This was at Sansapor, over 600 miles from Hollandia. By now some 120,000 Japanese were cut off, trapped in the "green hell" of the jungle in one of the worst climates in the world, and defenceless against malaria. It is understandable that, in face of this great success, MacArthur telegraphed to Eichelberger:

"The succession of surprises effected and the small losses suffered, the great extent of territory conquered and the casualties inflicted on the enemy, together with the large Japanese forces which have been isolated, all combine to make your operations of the past one and a half months models of strategical and tactical manoeuvres."

It should also be remembered that the death-rate in American hospitals was three per cent, whereas it was very much higher amongst the Japanese because of the appallingly unsanitary conditions under which they had to fight. MacArthur received Marshall's congratulations with justifiable satisfaction, but was even more pleased when the Pentagon announced that he was to get another corps, of five divisions, an extra air force, and 60 extra

Contrails of Fighters mark the sky during the "Marianas Turkey Shoot"

was the air attacks on Saipan, Tinian, and Guam in the Marianas.

The double offensive which had paid off for Nimitz at Tarawa was now working for MacArthur. Mitscher's bombers had an easy job of it over their objectives because the Biak affair had drawn off many fighters from the defence of the Marianas. Washington's misgivings were thus allayed by events.

The Marianas

As the Joint Chiefs-of-Staff directive of March 12 pointed out, the capture of the three islands mentioned above gave them a base for an attack on Mindanao in the Philippines. At Saipan, Army Air Force engineers would lay down the runways needed for the B-29 Superfortresses of the 20th Air Force to take off on their missions of destruction over the great industrial centres of the Japanese mainland. Operation "Forager", started on July 6, involved 535 warships and 127,571 men of the Marine Corps and the Army. Task Force 58 was followed by the Joint Expeditionary Force, Task Force 51, whose job it was to put ashore two corps of four divisions and one brigade:

1. V Amphibious Corps (Lieutenant-General Holland M. Smith: 2nd and 4th Marine Divisions);

2. III Amphibious Corps (Major-General Roy S. Geiger: 3rd Infantry Division and 1st Provisional Marine Brigade); and

3. floating reserve: 27th Division (Major-General Ralph Smith).

Admiral Spruance was C.-in-C., and Vice-Admiral Turner commanded the sea, air, and land forces involved in the landing. Both had recently been promoted. This powerful combination of

ships. What he had called the "stony-broke" war was a thing of the past.

The attack on Biak made the first dent in the Japanese defensive perimeter as described by the Imperial H.Q. directive commented on above. So Admiral Toyoda, who like the Americans had just formed a 1st Mobile Fleet (C.-in-C. Vice-Admiral Jisaburo Ozawa), resolved to attack MacArthur's flank. He despatched to the Moluccas an Attack Division (Vice-Admiral Matome Ugaki) consisting mainly of the giant battleships Yamato and Musashi, but on June 11, when it had scarcely reached its departure-point, it was suddenly ordered to abandon the operation and to rejoin Ozawa east of the Philippines. The reason

Aircraft drop supplies to the 503rd parachute regiment New Guinea.

than he had been in "Galvanic". This is shown by the number of fast carriers available to the 5th Fleet: 11 at the Gilberts, 12 at the Marshalls, and 15 at the Marianas.

Spruance thwarts Ozawa's plans...

American superiority in naval aircraft was over two to one. Spruance had 891, his adversary 430. The Japanese pilots, after their idleness at anchor in Tawitawi, had lost what little efficiency they had had. The Japanese carrier-force had two problems: it did not dare put out to sea because of the submarine threat; and there were no aerodromes near its base where its pilots could be trained. Ozawa's carriers did, it is true, have a greater range of action, but this had been achieved by the sacrifice of a certain amount of armour protection and a reduction in water-tight integrity, which rendered them very vulnerable.

Ozawa, in whom the historian Samuel Eliot Morison recognises "a scientific brain and a flair for trying new expedients, as well as a seaman's innate sense of what can be accomplished with ships", overlooked all these weaknesses in the hope of overcoming them by close collaboration with land-based aircraft from the Marianas and the organisation of a shuttle-service between his own and the "unsinkable carriers" of Guam and Rota. But this plan was thwarted by Spruance.

Moreover, Japanese strategy could no longer choose between offensive and defensive operations for, unless the Mobile Fleet were engaged, they would lose the Marianas, and the Philippines soon afterwards. In which case, Admiral Toyoda declared later:

"Even though the fleet should be left, the shipping lane to the

forces spelled the end of Japanese strategy as it had been conceived since the Washington Naval Conference of 1922. Then, when they had conceded a numerical superiority to the U.S. of five to three in battleships, the Japanese could still persuade themselves that their security was not at risk. In their opinion the bulk of the enemy's forces would be trapped and destroyed piecemeal in ambushes laid for them in the Marshall and Caroline Islands. The balance of strength would thus be in their favour in the Marianas. This turned out to be incorrect. In fact, far from losing strength as he advanced, Spruance was much stronger in Operation "Forager" south would be completely cut off so that the fleet, if it should come back to Japanese waters, could not obtain its fuel supply. If it should remain in southern waters, it could not receive supplies of ammunition and arms. There would be no sense in saving the fleet at the expense of the loss of the Philippines."

... and Ozawa reaches the Philippine Sea

This was why, when he heard about the bombing of the Marianas, Toyoda ordered Ozawa to put in action the plan for a counter-offensive which had been drawn up for this purpose. During the evening of June 15, Ozawa sailed into the Philippine Sea through the San Bernardino Strait and 24 hours later joined up with Ugaki's Attack Division. At 0008 hours on the 18th, he sent the following message to the Mobile Fleet:

"I humbly transmit to you the message I have just received from the Emperor via the Chief-of-Staff, Naval Section, Imperial G.H.Q.: 'This operation has immense bearing on the fate of the Empire.

It is hoped that the forces will exert their utmost and achieve as magnificent results as in the Battle of Tsushima.'"

There was, however, nothing in common between the American 5th Fleet and the Russian 2nd Pacific Squadron destroyed by Admiral Togo on May 27 and 28, 1905.

Spruance moves out

Patrolling off Tawitawi and at the exit of the San Bernardino Strait, Vice-Admiral Lockwood's submarines had signalled the approach of the Japanese Mobile Fleet and, with some

uncertainty, its composition. In view of the coming battle, Spruance called back his forces which had just been bombing the Bonin and Volcano Islands north of the Marianas, and redeployed his units. On the flanks of his four carrier task groups, still under Vice-Admiral Mitscher, he drew up a Battle Line under Vice-Admiral W. A. Lee: his seven fast battleships, four cruisers, and 13 destroyers. At 1415 hours on June 17 he defined his intentions to his immediate subordinates:

"Our air will first knock out enemy carriers, then will attack enemy battleships and cruisers to slow down or disable them. Battle line will destroy enemy fleet either by fleet action if the enemy elects to fight or by sinking slowed or crippled ships if enemy retreats. Action against the enemy must be pushed vigorously by all hands to ensure complete destruction of his fleet."

Spruance's intentions were thus purely offensive. He could not, however, go outside the parameters of his mission, which was to take, occupy, and defend Saipan, Tinian, and Guam. By giving chase to the enemy he would have left V Amphibious Corps' bridgehead unprotected and risked exposing it to attack from any Japanese force moving in from north or south. He therefore decided to sit back and wait a while.

The Japanese fleet advances

At dawn on June 19, the Japanese Mobile Fleet consisted of two detachments: a Van Force (Vice-Admiral Takeo Kurita) with three divisions, two of battleships and one of heavy cruisers, each protecting a light carrier, and 120 miles behind it a Main Body

First assault wave of US troops at New Guinea.

(Ozawa) composed of Forces "A" and "B", with six carriers, five of them fleet carriers. The Japanese sailed in against the wind: their planes were thus able to take off straight towards the enemy, with the return flight shorter than the outward one.

Between daybreak and 1445 hours, Ozawa made four raids on the 5th Fleet. These were all disastrous because of American superiority in training and in the quality of their aircraft. 373 of the 473 Japanese planes available (including floatplanes) took off and met 450 U.S. fighters, which massacred them. Those which escaped got caught in the massive A.A. fire of the Task Groups and the Battle Line. Those of the fourth wave which attempted to land at the airfield on Guam were destroyed in the air or so

badly damaged on landing (the runways being pitted with bomb craters) that none of them ever took off again. Only 130 Japanese planes returned to their ships. There was no compensation for the Japanese as the U.S. forces lost only 18 fighters and 12 bombers and suffered only slight damage to the carrier Bunker Hill and the battleship South Dakota. The 5th Fleet lost altogether 58 men killed, including 27 pilots. Worse still for Ozawa, at 0910 hours the submarine Albacore (Commander J. W. Blanchard) put a torpedo into the fleet carrier Taiho (29,300 tons), Vice-Admiral Ozawa's flagship. Then at 1220 hours the submarine Cavalla (Lieutenant-Commander H. J. Kossler) scored three hits on the carrier Shokaku; she sank towards 1730 in the afternoon with 22 of her planes, which had just returned, on board. Both the Shokaku and the Taiho were lost because of explosions of the fumes from the fuel taken on at Tarakan. Damage to the Taiho was negligible, but a damage-control officer unfortunately gave the order to ventilate the ship and the petroleum fumes swept through from stem to stern. This led to a colossal explosion, as a result of which the ship sank immediately.

Twilight pursuit

Ozawa transferred his flag to the heavy cruiser Haguro and, misinformed about Japanese losses and misled by exaggerated reports by his own pilots of U.S. casualties, pressed on with his attack regardless. There is no doubt that the remainder of the Japanese fleet would have been wiped out in the course of June 20 if Spruance's aerial reconnaissance had spotted it in time, but it failed to do so, despite the beautiful weather. It was 1600 hours

US Marines advance against heavy enemy fire, Saipan.

before a plane sighted the Japanese "250 miles" (it was in fact over 300) north-north-west of Task Force 58. Despite the distance and the lateness of the hour, Spruance turned his carriers into the wind and sent up 85 fighters, 77 dive-bombers, and 54 torpedo-bombers inside ten minutes.

The sun was sinking below the horizon when the Americans saw the fighter screen protecting the Mobile Fleet. Each Japanese ship then took a separate zig-zag course and opened up with all its guns. Forty Japanese planes were shot down for a loss to the Americans of 20, but only a small carrier, the Hiyo, was sunk. Meanwhile Mitscher was sailing full steam ahead to save his planes as much milage as possible. To get them back on board at

2000 hours, Task Force 58 turned up-wind and, in spite of the submarine danger, turned on all their landing lights. A few hours later, on board the cruiser Montpelier; Leading Seaman James J. Fahey noted in his invaluable diary:

"It was a great decision to make and everyone thought the world of Admiral Marc Mitscher for doing this. This would make it easier for our pilots to land, and if they did hit the water they could be saved. The big carriers were all lighted so the pilots could see where to land, a lot of our destroyers were left behind to pick the men out of the water. I saw one pilot on the wing of his plane waving his shirt. There were so many lights it must have been hard to land on the carriers. A Jap plane also tried to land on one of our carriers. Our planes continued to land as we continued on our way after the Jap fleet. It was quite a sight to see all the ships lit up, flares and rafts in the water and some planes crashing into the water, and pilots and crews also in the water. You could see the planes circle and then land on the carriers. A great job was done by everyone to save our pilots' lives. The Japs would never do anything like this."

Even so, out of 176 planes which got back to Task Force 58, 80 ran out of fuel and fell into the sea or crash-landed. Thanks to Mitscher's initiative, 101 crew were picked up. Another 59 were saved on the following day, making the losses for the 20th 49. Ozawa was informed that only 35 out of his 473 planes were left, and so he broke off contact.

Japanese Prisoners Aitape, New Guinea.

A catastrophe for the Japanese

The Philippine Sea was thus the graveyard of the Japanese naval air arm. The Japanese carriers, bereft of planes and pilots, were like rifles without cartridges. At the cost of 130 of the 956 planes his task force had at dawn on June 19, and of 138 sailors and airmen killed or missing, Spruance had thus scored a victory the consequences of which were to last until the Japanese capitulation of September 2, 1945.

The fact remains that a number of Spruance's subordinate officers and fellow-commanders, who did not know of the loss of the Taiho, however, expressed their disappointment that the Mobile Fleet had not been destroyed, a result of what they considered excessive caution on Spruance's part. Nimitz and King backed him up, however. Perhaps by so doing they were merely vindicating themselves in that this incomplete victory could have been the result of their somewhat restrictive instruction to take, occupy, and defend Saipan, Tinian, and Guam. Be that as it may, some months later Admiral W. F. Halsey found that the order sending him to Leyte contained the following paragraph:

"In case opportunity for destruction of major portion of the enemy fleet offers or can be created, such destruction becomes the primary task."

The disaster of the Philippine Sea was soon to be followed by the loss of the Marianas Islands: Tinian, Saipan and Guam. A consequence of these defeats was the forced resignation of General

Tojo as Prime Minister.

On July 18, 1944, Hirohito appointed General Kuniaki Koiso as Tojo's successor. The new Prime Minister had been Governor of Korea, had left the Army in 1938, and had the reputation of being a moderate. The War Ministry went to Field-Marshal Sugiyama, the Navy to Admiral Yonai. Shigemitsu, who had taken part in the conspiracy within the Tojo cabinet, remained Foreign Minister.

The search for peace

The Emperor ended his audience with the new Prime Minister with the following words: "You will need to collaborate to put an end to the war in Asia and I recommend you not to upset Russia."

In guarded terms the Emperor was therefore ordering Koiso and Yonai to attempt a negotiated settlement with the United States and Great Britain. The new Navy Minister saw the situation in the same light. When he had asked Admiral Toyoda: "Can we hold out until the end of the year?" the reply was: "It will in all probability be very difficult."

When we realise that the Japanese language is full of circumlocutions and delicate shades of meaning we see what that meant. The army chiefs had still to be reckoned with, however, and they refused to admit that any negotiated settlement could be compatible with the Emperor's honour, of which they considered themselves the absolute and final judges, regardless of their devotion to his person. "Divine Presence" was one of the Emperor's attributes, but for the military man this was only on condition that he took no part in major policy decisions. Even if the army leaders had been more foreseeing than this, General Koiso would still have found it just as difficult to overcome this obstacle. Potter and Nimitz note this clearly:

"On the Allied side, the goal of unconditional surrender set by Roosevelt and Churchill at Casablanca forbade the proffering of terms which might have served as bases for negotiation."

And so the road led inevitably to Hiroshima and Nagasaki.

Tanks and troops of the 162nd Infantry Regiment Hollandia New Guinea.

The so-called "March on Delhi", the Japanese offensive against the British IV Corps on the Tiddim-Imphal-Kohima front which started rolling when Lieutenant-General G. Yanagida's 33rd Division crossed the Chindwin in force on the night of March 7–8, was the brainchild of Lieutenant-General Renya Mutaguchi, aged 55.

To the Japanese it was known as the "U-GO" offensive and its limited objective was to forestall a British offensive by attacking and destroying the British base at Imphal, thus strengthening the Japanese defence of Burma.

A subsidiary objective was, with the use of the Indian National Army division raised and commanded by the plausible and resourceful Subhas Chandra Bhose, to "exercise political control over India". This was to be achieved by encouraging and supporting dissident anti-British elements, who had in the previous year created a most serious situation in Bengal and Bihar by their widespread sabotage of bridges, communications, and airfields. As it happened Chandra Bhose stayed comfortably in Rangoon and the I.N.A. division, which had the strength of only a brigade (totalling about 7,000 men), had little effect on either the battle or the political situation.

The date of the "U-GO" offensive was timed to phase in with the successful outcome of Major-General T. Sakurai's "HA-GO" offensive in the Arakan. The latter's purpose was to draw off the Allied reserve divisions to the Arakan prior to Mutaguchi's attack on Imphal. This task Sakurai's 55th Division had successfully achieved for, by the end of February 1944, six divisions (5th, 7th, 25th, 26th, 36th, and 81st West African), a parachute brigade,

and a special service (commando) brigade, had been drawn into that theatre. This concentration, coupled with the extensive use of air supply, had certainly foiled Sakurai's raid after three weeks of hard fighting. But Mutaguchi should have crossed the Chindwin in mid-February as planned in order to take the maximum advantage of Sakurai's feint.

Unfortunately Lieutenant-General M. Yamauchi's 15th Division, which Mutaguchi intended to use for the direct assault on Imphal, had become stuck in Siam. It was not until February 11, after Mutaguchi himself had signalled Field-Marshal Count Terauchi, commander of the Southern Army at Singapore, that the 15th Division started to concentrate in Burma, arriving ill-equipped, ill-fed, and ill-tempered.

This division had been training in northern Siam and some of its units had been improving the Chiengmai-Toungoo road as an alternative route to the much bombed Burma-Siam railway. Assisted by ten motor transport companies, it had marched the 700-mile long road from Chiengmai to Shwebo via Kentung and Mandalay in order to toughen itself up and prepare itself for its task ahead.

D-day for the "U-GO" offensive was fixed for March 15, by which time the 15th Division must not only be re-equipped but have moved to its start line between Paungbyin and Sittaung on the Chindwin, as well as organising its communications forward from Indaw and Wuntho on the railway via Pinlebu.

The other two divisions in Mutaguchi's 15th Army were in a much better state. The 33rd Division had operated for many years in China and had taken part from the start in the conquest of Burma as well as combating the first Chindit operation in 1943. This division, advancing initially along comparatively good roads, would carry with it all the armour and heavy artillery (4th Tank Regiment, 1st Anti-Tank Battalion, 3rd and 18th Heavy Field Artillery Regiments) that the Japanese could muster for this attack.

The 31st Division (Lieutenant-General K. Sato), whose task was the unenviable one of advancing from Homalin and Tamanthi on the upper reaches of the Chindwin river, and then over a series of parallel ridges (reaching a height of over 7,000 feet) to Jessami and Kohima, had previously operated only in China, although some of its units had been stationed on islands in the Pacific. It had arrived in Burma between June and September 1943 and had immediately been sent to the Chindwin front, where it had crossed swords with the battle-experienced 20th Indian Division (Major-General D.D. Gracey). The 31st Division had had, therefore, plenty of time to get inured to the conditions in that area. It would operate on a mule and horse transport basis, trusting on a tenuous 100-mile long line of communications from Mawlu and Indaw on the railway to Tamanthi and Homalin, supported by a three-week reserve of food, ammunition, and fodder built up on the line of the Chindwin.

Mutaguchi, "the victor of Singapore", had previously commanded the 18th Division in north Burma and had been most impressed by the activities of the Chindits and their leader, Brigadier Wingate, whom he held in high regard. Mutaguchi had, with some difficulty, sold his plan to knock out IV Corps by a three-pronged, three-divisional thrust against the 200-mile

Allied patrol on Imphal road, scene of recent Japanese offensive.

road leading down from the Brahmaputra valley parallel to the Chindwin. Prime Minister Tojo and Count Terauchi agreed to this gamble only because they needed some offensive success to offset the disasters which had been occurring in the Pacific. They then agreed only with the proviso that it should be combined with an attempt to start widespread insurrection in East India with the cooperation of Subhas Chandra Bhose's Indian National Army, on which they placed great hopes of success.

Lieutenant-General M. Kawabe, commanding the Burma Area Army, was sceptical of the whole plan and had orders to prevent Mutaguchi from overreaching himself. Lieutenant-General Tazoe, commanding the 5th Air Division, had no faith in Mutaguchi's plan whatsoever. He was apprehensive of what the Allied airborne forces (the Chindits) would do, for his reconnaissance aircraft had shown they were ready to be sent in again. He pointed out to Mutaguchi that he would be totally incapable of helping him with air supply once he had crossed the Chindwin.

Mutaguchi's plan was for the 33rd Division, with the bulk of his armour and artillery, to advance from its bridgehead at Kalewa and to attack and surround the 17th Indian Division (Major-General D.T. Cowan) at Tiddim and Tongzang. Leaving a small containing force, the 33rd Division would push forward with all speed northwards to the Imphal plain, where it would also cut the Bishenpur Track running west to Silchar. One regiment, under Major-General T. Yamamoto, would meanwhile advance north from Kalemyo up the Kabaw valley and open a road through to support the 15th Division, bringing most of the wheeled and track vehicles with it.

The 33rd Division would start its advance one week before D-day, when the 15th and 31st Divisions would cross the Chindwin.

The 15th Division's task was to cross the Chindwin near Thaungdut and advance on tracks via Ukhrul to cut the Dimapur road north of Imphal near Kanglatongbi. It would also detail one column to contain the 20th Division (Gracey) east of Palel. With the 33rd Division, its final objective was to overrun the rich Imphal plain, destroy IV Corps, and capture the airfields and a vast quantity of supplies.

The 31st Division had the more arduous task of advancing 70 to 100 miles along footpaths from the riverine villages of Tamanthi and Homalin, through the Naga Hills, and over a series of bare mountain ranges to capture Kohima, a small, obscure village and staging post on a 4,000-foot pass on the Dimapur–Imphal road. Whether it would exploit its success from there by attacking the undefended railhead at Dimapur depended on circumstances.

Mutaguchi hoped that the whole operation would be resolved within three weeks, by which time he also hoped to have road communications functioning from Kalewa via Palel to Imphal and north to Kohima.

The command set-up in Burma as far as 14th Army was concerned was rather top heavy. The Supreme Commander, Lord Louis Mountbatten, gave his orders to General Giffard, commanding 11th Army Group, who commanded only one army, Lieutenant-General Slim's 14th Army. 14th Army initially had under command XV Corps (Lieutenant-General A.F.P. Christison) in the Arakan, IV Corps (Lieutenant-General G.A.P. Scoones), the Northern Combat Area Command (Lieutenant-General J. W. Stilwell), and Special Force (Major-General O.C. Wingate). Later XXXIII Corps (Lieutenant-General M.G.N. Stopford) was formed in the Brahmaputra valley to counter the Japanese advance, and XV Corps came under the direct command of General Sir George Giffard's 11th Army Group.

Slim had not been deceived by the violence of Sakurai's Arakan attack and his countering the threat by the fly-in of overwhelming numbers, coupled with his strict orders that all units should stand firm if their communications were cut and await supply by air, had converted what might have been a disaster in the Arakan to a morale-raising victory.

Slim realised from Intelligence reports that IV Corps might suffer similar long-range penetration attacks, but he thought that these could not be in a strength greater than two regiments. He made his plans accordingly. On the night of March 5–6 he allowed the Chindit airborne operation to start its fly-in across the Chindwin to block the Japanese communications facing General Stilwell's forces (N.C.A.C.), in accordance with the orders of the Combined Chiefs-of-Staff.

IV Corps consisted of three divisions (17th, 20th, and 23rd) and the 254th Indian Tank Brigade (with Shermans and Grants). The 17th Division, after its retreat from Burma in 1942, had stayed for two years patrolling in the 7,000-foot Tiddim Hills, 100 miles south of Imphal. This light division consisted of two, mainly Gurkha, brigades on a mule/jeep transport basis.

The 20th Division was based on Palel and Tamu south-east of Imphal and patrolled towards the Chindwin.

The 23rd Division (Major-General O.L. Roberts) was in reserve at Imphal. Lieutenant-General Scoones, who had commanded IV Corps since its formation, was a clever, quiet, forceful personality who achieved results through efficiency and attention to detail rather than by flamboyant leadership. With him his subordinates would know that everything would be in its place and up to strength.

Scoones' plan, which had been approved by Slim, was, on being attacked, to withdraw his two forward divisions back to the wide open Imphal plain, where he would be able to bring to bear his superiority in tanks heavy artillery, and close air support, which could outgun and destroy anything that the Japanese could bring over the hills and across the Chindwin against them. He would then have three divisions, with a promise of a fourth to be flown in, to combat the Japanese raid. The vital factor in his plan was when to give the order for the 17th Division to start its 100-mile retirement back from Tiddim to Imphal.

Slim planned to fly in the 5th Indian Division (Major-General H.R. Briggs) from the Arakan as soon as news of an attack in strength was confirmed. The 50th Parachute Brigade (Brigadier M.R.J. Hope-Thompson) was due to be flown into Imphal and directed towards Ukhrul. Scoones planned to fly out all unnecessary administrative personnel and the very large number of engineers and their civilian working force who were engaged on

Gurkhas cut bamboo stakes to protect their positions, Imphal area.

improving communications and airfields within the Imphal area. In fact over 40,000 "unwanted mouths" were flown out as the battle progressed.

IV Corps consisted eventually of the 5th, 17th, 20th, and 23rd Indian Divisions, the 50th Indian Parachute Brigade, and the 254th Indian Tank Brigade (Shermans and Grants), comprising 49 infantry battalions (nine British, 24 Indian, and 16 Gurkha), and 120 tanks. Besides this, IV Corps had the 8th Medium Regiment, Royal Artillery, with 5.5-inch guns, as well as the usual complement of divisional artillery and engineers. In all there were about 120,000 men, excluding constructional engineers and Royal Air Force.

The strength of the Japanese 15th Army which crossed the Chindwin was 84,280 Japanese and 7,000 Indians. A further 4,000 reinforcements arrived during operations. The Japanese divided each division into three columns of varying size and composition, according to their tasks, but the total number of units which can be compared with those of IV Corps were as follows: nine infantry regiments, totalling 26 battalions (one battalion of the 15th Division had been sent back to deal with the landing of the airborne forces, but was later returned to the 15th Division during its attack on Imphal); two heavy artillery regiments; and one tank regiment.

Besides these there were divisional artillery, with much of it on a light mountain pack basis, and three engineer regiments, which were often used as infantry.

The British XXXIII Corps at its maximum strength consisted of two divisions (British 2nd and 7th Indian, under Major-Generals J.M.L. Grover and F.W. Messervy respectively), the 149th Regiment, Royal Armoured Corps, the 23rd (L.R.P.) Brigade (Brigadier L.E.C.M. Perowne), the 3rd Special Service (Commando) Brigade (Brigadier W.I. Nonweiler), and the Lushai Brigade (Brigadier P.C. Marindin), totalling about 75,000 troops, including 34 infantry battalions (20 British, 11 Indian, and three Gurkha).

Yanagida started his advance to attack on the night of March 7–8. The 215th Regiment went up the high mountains to Fort White and crossed the Manipur river to get into a position west of the 17th Indian Division's position at Tiddim and Tongzang.

The 214th Regiment marched northwest and advanced directly on Tongzang. Both regiments formed blocks across the Tiddim-Imphal road. Cowan, commanding the 17th Indian Division, had not told his brigadiers that there were plans for withdrawal, so on March 13, when he got Scoones's order to withdraw, his brigades had to have time to see that the orders reached every man. This meant a 24-hour delay. This particular division, consisting of a preponderance of Gurkhas, was well trained and had great confidence in itself and its quiet commander. Withdrawal continued according to plan and at each road-block the Gurkhas put into operation plans they had rehearsed and the Japanese blocks were removed without great difficulty, but with considerable loss to the Japanese.

However, Scoones was apprehensive of how successfully the 17th Division would be able to carry out this 100-mile long withdrawal on a road through high hills and where there were ambush positions every few hundred yards. So he committed some of his reserve division, the 23rd, which he had moved to Torbung. The 37th and 49th Brigades, with a squadron of tanks, were moved forward to Milestone 100.

Yanagida pressed on, but his troops were losing their momentum and after the fourth block across the road had been successfully removed by the British forces, Yanagida became depressed. On the night of March 23, after receiving many casualties, Yanagida sent a rather panicky signal to Mutaguchi implying that his position was hopeless. Yanagida had been appalled at the success of the Sherman and Grant medium tanks, against which neither his artillery nor his anti-tank guns seemed to have any affect.

After an exchange of furious signals Mutaguchi decided to remove Yanagida and sent for a successor. It must be emphasised that this took place at the beginning of the campaign and affected the command and consequently the morale of the division on which the success of the whole operation depended.

Major-General Yamamoto's column which, it will be remembered, had the preponderance of Japanese armour, advanced quickly and surely up the Kabaw valley until by March 11 it had reached a position at Maw on the right flank of Gracey's 20th Indian Division. Gracey had taken his brigade commanders into his confidence about what action the division would take when Scoones gave the order to withdraw. So his brigades knew exactly what to do when he ordered them to destroy unnecessary stores, disengage, move back, and reform on the Shenam Heights just east of Palel. This withdrawal took place in good order and without a hitch, but was followed up by Yamamoto. Heavy fighting soon took place on the Palel road at a point that became known as Nippon Hill.

Moving further north, Yamauchi's 15th Division crossed the Chindwin on the night of March 15–16 and moved quickly up the hills towards Ukhrul. According to plan he also sent a detachment to make contact with Yamamoto's column on the Palel Road. By March 21 Yamamoto was in contact with the 50th Parachute Brigade at Ukhrul, where it had taken over from the 23rd Division's 49th Brigade, which in turn had been moved to assist the 17th Division. All this time it must be remembered that Mutaguchi was in Maymyo, 200 miles to the east, the pleasant hill station in which he had set up his headquarters. It was from this viewpoint that he sent signals exhorting his three divisional commanders to greater effort.

The 15th Division's orders were to bypass Ukhrul and move towards the hills north of the Imphal plain to seize Kanglatongbi.

Further north still, Sato's 31st Division which, having been in the area for many months, had had time to reconnoitre the routes over the hills, and done remarkably well. Crossing the Chindwin between Homalin and Tamanthi on the night of March 15–16, his left-hand column reached Ukhrul, where it made contact with Yamauchi's forces. Whilst Yamauchi pushed on, Sato's left-hand column, under the command of Major-General Shigesburo Miyazaki, made contact with the Indian Parachute Brigade at Sangshak near Ukhrul. After pushing out the paratroops, Miyazaki advanced north-west and set up a road block at Maram on March 27, a few miles south of Kohima.

Meanwhile Sato's 58th and 124th Regiments advanced on

Jessami. Jessami was weakly held by the Assam Regiment and was captured on April 1.

Kohima itself had originally been defended by Brigadier D.F.W. Warren's 161st Brigade of the 5th Division, which had been flown up from the Arakan to Dimapur. When Lieutenant-General Stopford took command of the area with his XXXIII Corps, he unfortunately withdrew Brigadier Warren from Kohima to protect Dimapur itself, where there were 60,000 unarmed rear echelon troops looking after the stores and administration. This move left Kohima virtually unprotected. Sato continued his advance and by April 15 Kohima itself was invested.

Slim's calculations had been that not more than one Japanese regiment could be maintained at Kohima. This was, in fact, the case and Sato's men were to suffer for it later. But in the meantime this attack by a whole division threw the British defence plans out of gear.

The battles which followed centred around the sieges of Imphal and Kohima, but for the British, success depended also upon the co-ordination of forces in the whole of Burma, a formidable logistical problem.

Scoones had mapped out a very sensible defence of the Imphal plain. He formed fortresses or "boxes" around each area where there were stores or airfields, and had detailed a commander with staff in charge of that area with a force to defend it. This worked well, but when pressure from the Japanese intensified he had to reduce the size of these areas and give up some of the stores, which then fell into Japanese hands. By this time he had four divisions and the parachute brigade with the formidable 254th Medium

Tank Brigade to fight his battle. He also had 27 squadrons of fighters and fighter-bombers at short call to harass and destroy the Japanese, who were better targets now that they were emerging into the open plain. It must also be remembered that on the high ground the hills were bare and Sato's 31st Division suffered heavily from air attack when caught out in the open at Litan during its advance on Kohima.

Into the trap

In the Brahmaputra valley XXXIII Corps, whose nucleus was the 2nd British Division (which had originally been the theatre reserve and had been training for operations in Sumatra or Malaya), was now forming fast. The 2nd Division had too many vehicles for the type of country, but as it advanced it soon learnt how to fight with only one road as its main axis. Stopford, realising his mistake in withdrawing Warren's 161st Brigade, sent them back to the Kohima area, where a tiny garrison of the Royal West Kents and Assam Rifles was holding out gallantly.

It was now five weeks since Sato had crossed the Chindwin, and his supplies were beginning to dry up. He was faced by a series of problems: exceptionally difficult terrain, poor communications and the activities of the Chindits who had destroyed the Japanese railway supply lines and cut off 300 trucks from Sato.

Sato signalled Mutaguchi that he was running out of supplies and was having to eat his mules. He suggested that he should start retiring whilst he still had some pack animals left. Mutaguchi was appalled by this message and sent some extremely rude signals to the conscientious Sato.

Meanwhile, the Chindit 23rd (L.R.P.) Brigade had been put under Stopford's command. He gave it the task of making a wide sweep to the east to get behind the Japanese 31st Division and to advance all the way to Ukhrul. The eight columns of the brigade pushed on along the footpaths over the high ridge with their mule transport and with supply by air. Many small actions were fought and although it was not possible in this country with its many paths to "cut" communications, the force threatened Sato's communications to such an extent that he told Mutaguchi that he must withdraw.

Mutaguchi was going through a bad time. He had replaced Yanagida with Major-General N. Tanaka, who was a tough, resilient, earthy soldier who had fought in north China. Mutaguchi had no luck with the 15th Division either, as the divisional commander, Yamauchi, died of malaria. He was replaced by Lieutenant-General U. Shibata, a man, it was said, "with an ox-like presence".

The Japanese collapse

As the fighting for Kohima went on, Mutaguchi was issuing orders of the day appealing to all ranks, saying that the throne of the Emperor depended on them and so on. But this did not move the intelligent and worldly-wise Sato. Mutaguchi sent staff officers to see him, but Sato took no notice of them. On April 30 Sato signalled again, pointing out the hopelessness of his position. These signals continued until on June 1 Sato signalled "Propose retreating from Kohima with rearguard." Mutaguchi replied

"Retreat and I will court-marshal you." Sato replied "Do as you please I will bring you down with me." This gives some idea of the division and state of mind of the Japanese force commanders, who were fighting against odds at Kohima and Imphal. Sato was quite adamant as he saw his men staggering back half naked, without ammunition and weapons, and relying on bamboo shoots and roots for their sustenance. He was determined that Mutaguchi should be brought back to Tokyo for court-marshal for basic neglect of administration.

Sato left Miyazaki with 750 of his best and fittest men to form a rearguard south of Kohima, which had now been cleared by the 2nd Division, and retreated. The rest of his division, all supplies having been stopped by the Chindits, ceased to exist and melted away.

Around Imphal, however, very heavy fighting continued. With their two new divisional commanders, the 15th Division and 33rd Divisions were attacking Scoones from all directions, and it was only as a result of the skill and high morale of his divisions, coupled with the technical superiority of his tanks, the R.A.F., and the 8th Medium Artillery Regiment, that he could keep at bay the fanatical assaults of these Japanese.

It is worth digressing here to point out that defence against well-trained soldiers who are quite prepared to take part in suicidal attacks is quite different from defence against reasonable men who, when they see a situation is hopeless, will withdraw or surrender. This was one reason why commanders who came from the European theatre took some time to settle down to the new type of tactics. Their enemy in this theatre had not only to be outmanoeuvred, beaten, and have their weapons overcome, but they themselves had to be destroyed one by one.

From a distance, in London and Washington, it appeared that IV Corps was not making sufficient effort to fight its way out, and some criticism was received on this count, but IV Corps had also to expend and disperse men to protect airfields and stores against suicide attacks and so was not quite free to launch the strong offensive towards Ukhrul which it had been ordered to make. Both the 20th and 23rd Divisions had been ordered to capture Ukhrul, but both had made little progress.

The 2nd Division continued its advance down the road and on June 22 contact was made between the two corps at Milestone 109, just north of the Imphal plain. Stopford had advanced 70 miles from Kohima but Scoones had fought less than ten miles uphill out of the plain. The monsoon was now in full spate, but Slim ordered the two corps to pursue. This was easier said than done. The Japanese 15th Division, suffering severely from disease and lack of supplies, as the Chindits had cut their communications east to the railway, was in a very bad way. But it managed to hold out at Ukhrul and had prevented the pincer movement which Slim had designed to cut it off.

The 33rd Division, with its new commander, was in better shape and was fighting well on the roads running south to Kalemyo and Kalewa.

The 19th Indian Division had joined the British 2nd Division in its advance south so that the Allied forces had managed to collect the equivalent of nine divisions with overwhelming air superiority against the Japanese three divisions and the I.N.A.

brigade. As the monsoon wore on, the Japanese defeat became more complete as a result of disease and lack of supplies. The British have the reputation of not being good in pursuit, and there was undoubtedly a slackening in follow-up, but the British commanders felt that the monsoon was completing their victory. Chandra Bhose's I.N.A. melted away, whilst Sato returned accusing Mutaguchi of negligence and incompetence, stating that his division had received no ammunition or supplies for six weeks. Mutaguchi had on May 15 moved his headquarters to Tamu, and it was only then when he saw the condition of his men and experienced the absolute dominance of the air by the R.A.F. that he realised the extent to which he was being defeated. Of the 88,000 Japanese (including reinforcements) who had crossed the Irrawaddy, 53,505 became casualties, including 30,502 killed, missing, or dead of disease.

Victory at Kohima/Imphal would probably not have been possible without absolute air superiority, air supply, and close air support.

Deliveries to IV Corps on the Imphal plain between April 18 and June 30 totalled 18,824 tons of stores of all sorts and at least 12,561 personnel. On their return flights the transport aircraft (R.A.F. and U.S.A.A.F.) evacuated 13,000 casualties and 43,000 non-combatants. The total number of reinforcements carried is difficult to calculate, as space was always made available to take in extra men. But 1,540 sorties were flown to move the 5th Division, the 7th Division (33rd and 89th Brigades), and the 4th Brigade of the 2nd Division to the Central Front. The Lushai Brigade and the 23rd Brigade were wholly, and XXXIII Corps was partially, supplied by air during their advance.

Between March 10 and July 30, R.A.F. fighters of the 3rd T.A.F. flew 18,860 sorties and those of the U.S.A.A.F. 10,800 sorties, losing 130 R.A.F. and 40 U.S. A.A.F. aircraft. The majority of these 29,660 sorties flown was for close air support of troops on the ground. During the same period the J.A.A.F. flew 1,750 sorties.

This gives some idea of the Allied dominance of the air and the importance of the construction of all-weather airfields on the ground in this campaign.

In spite of their evident superiority in numbers, all ranks of the British and Indian units had fought hard and very well, and had learnt to trust each other. British and Indian casualties during the battles of Imphal and Kohima were just under 16,700, of which approximately a quarter were incurred at Kohima in spite of strict medical and anti-malarial precautions, sickness caused more than 12 times the number of battle casualties, although many of those who went sick could return to their units.

After Imphal was relieved on June 22, Slim reformed his forces on that front. IV Corps, with the 17th and 20th Divisions who had been holding the line for two years, was withdrawn to India for a refit. The 50th Parachute Brigade was also withdrawn. Slim moved his own headquarters into Imphal and ordered Stopford's XXXIII Corps to continue the pursuit of the Japanese 33rd Division southwards, XXXIII Corps now consisted of the British 2nd, 5th and 20th Indian, and 11th East African Divisions. Movement through the mountains in the monsoon, coupled with extensive demolitions by the Japanese 33rd Division, slowed the British advance to a snail's pace, so that the Chindwin was not reached or crossed until early December, by which time Northern Combat Area Command's British 86th Division (Festing) had advanced down the railway from Mogaung to within 100 miles north of Mandalay. This "turned" the front of the Japanese facing XXXIII Corps so that the former swung back facing north, with their axis on Kalewa.

The Japanese 15th Army had been beaten. The Allies were now on the dry plains of Burma where tanks, artillery, and aircraft could be used to the maximum effect. The time was ripe for the ejection of the Japanese from Burma. The orders given to the Supreme Commander, Lord Louis Mountbatten, by the Chiefs-of-Staff had been fulfilled. He now received new orders to drive the Japanese out of Burma completely, by advancing on Mandalay and then on Rangoon.

Scene of some of the bloodiest fighting at Kohima.

The return of General Douglas MacArthur to the Philippines was assured. As his aircraft climbed above Oahu in the afternoon sunlight he turned to an aide and said, "We've sold it!"

He had sold his plan for an invasion of the Philippines to President Roosevelt and Admiral Nimitz. On board the Baltimore and at a private house near Pearl Harbor they had spent the afternoon of July 26, 1944 and the morning of the following day in discussion. Finally they agreed that both sound strategy and national honour required the liberation of the Philippines.

It was further agreed that "the Philippines should be recovered with ground and air power then available in the Western Pacific" as they were not going to wait until the defeat of Germany.

Nimitz was to add that "from hindsight I think that decision was correct". But at the time there were two strongly-held strategic concepts of the war in the Pacific.

In the autumn of 1943, MacArthur had submitted his views for the future to the Joint Chiefs-of-Staff. After neutralising the Japanese air base in Rabaul by capturing the neighbouring base of Kavieng, and establishing himself further up the New Guinea coast at Hollandia and Aitape, he wished to strike north at Mindanao in the southern Philippines, and thence if possible at Luzon. These operations depended on a clear superiority of air and sea power over the Japanese in the area. They would probably require the presence of the main American fleet, as well as the other naval forces in the south Pacific.

With these forces MacArthur felt that he could be in Mindanao in December 1944, and Luzon the following spring. With his existing forces he was committed to a subsidiary rôle.

But in addition to these strategic considerations there was an emotional tie with the Philippines for MacArthur.

As military adviser to the Philippine Army he had created and trained it on the model of the Swiss Army.

When the Japanese landed 200,000 men in December 1941, MacArthur led a mixed American and Filipino army of about half that number. Fighting a defensive battle, he retreated to the Bataan peninsula and the island of Corregidor.

In the spring of 1942 Roosevelt ordered MacArthur to Canberra as C.-in-C. of the newly-formed S. W. Pacific Area. He was reluctant to go, but obeyed the order, and when he arrived in Australia promised "I came through and I shall return." He had thought that the Allies could mount an attack to relieve the Bataan garrison before it was overwhelmed by the Japanese, but now he felt that this promise was true for the whole of the Philippines.

Now MacArthur held an unusual position in the American military hierarchy. Unlike other senior commanders, he had not for some time had any direct connection with the War Department, yet he was considerably senior to any other serving officer, having retired as a Chief-of-Staff of the U.S. Army in 1935, when Marshall held the rank of Colonel. His background and his own self-confidence did not incline him to act as a subordinate in the manner of the other commanders.

A pronounced consciousness of his position, and the political importance which it fostered, gave to his relations with Washington something of the flavour of an independent power. But in service circles Admiral Leahy commented that "the

General Douglas MacArthur, President Franklin D Roosevelt, Admiral Chester W Nimitz aboard USS Baltimore.

mention of the name of MacArthur seemed to generate more heat than light".

He had not been to America since 1935, did not meet any of the American chiefs-of-staff until December 1943, had not received a direct communication from the President since assuming command of the South-West Pacific Area, and at the end of 1943 had never met Admiral Nimitz, his colleague in the Central Pacific.

Added to this difference of personalities there was the natural rivalry, of the Army and Navy which was brought out by the two proposed plans.

The Navy's plan: Formosa the goal

Admiral King, supported by Admiral Nimitz, based his planning on the experience of the fighting in New Guinea and the Solomon Islands. He definitely considered it "essential to avoid as long as possible fighting the Japanese army in any land area where they could delay … operations". American strength lay at sea and in the air, and not in slow and expensive fighting in jungle and urban areas.

When MacArthur took his leave on July 27, he assured the President that despite the differences between himself and Nimitz there was no cause for concern; agreement was near.

There were still differences between General MacArthur and Admiral Nimitz as to the best strategy for winning the war but the two sides had reached agreement. Leahy was later to assert that "the agreement… and the President's familiarity with the situation at this conference were to be of great value in preventing an unnecessary invasion of Japan which the planning staffs of the Joint Chiefs and the War Department were advocating, regardless of the loss of life that would result from an attack on Japan's forces in their own country."

Despite this top-level agreement, the J.C.S. continued to discuss the Pacific strategy. It was a short while later, on September 1, 1944, that Rear-Admiral Forrest Sherman, Admiral Nimitz's chief planner, confronted them. He said that it was high time a decision was reached, and that even a bad one would be better than none. Central Pacific armed forces had no directive for anything beyond the Palaus objective, which was due in two weeks. Admiral King still opposed Luzon, which he said would slow up the war for mere sentimental reasons (earlier he had dismissed MacArthur's plans as "desires and visions").

The plans, however, had won a powerful ally in General Marshall, who appreciated the argument about national honour, and also that Luzon would be easier to capture than Formosa. MacArthur had warned the J.C.S. that if they left the 16 million population of the Philippines to "wither on the vine" until the end of the war with Japan, they would not only inflict unpredictable hardships on the loyal Filipinos, but also cause all Asia to lose faith in American honour.

The J.C.S. planners worked out a timetable to be presented to the "Octagon" Combined Chiefs-of-Staff conference at Quebec on September 11, 1944:

1. September 15, South-West Pacific Forces occupy Morotai; Central Pacific forces occupy Peleliu October 5; occupy Yap, with Ulithi to follow.

2. October 15, South-West Pacific Forces occupy Salebaboe Island; November 15, land at Sarangani Bay, Mindanao; December 20, at Leyte.

3. South-West Pacific and Central Pacific forces then combine to occupy either (1) Luzon, to secure Manila by February 20, or (2) Formosa and Amoy on the China coast by March 1, 1945.

But as with many of the best laid plans, this timetable was scrambled within a week.

Task Force 38, under Admiral Halsey, left Eniwetok on August 28, 1944, to bomb Yap, the Palaus, and Mindanao, and make a one-group diversionary strike on the Bonin Islands. The aim was to destroy Japanese air forces which might challenge the forthcoming landings on Morotai and Peleliu, and to deceive the enemy as to the next target. The Palaus were bombed on September 6–8, Mindanao airstrips near Sarangani Bay on September 9–10. These attacks were unopposed, and this caused Halsey to cancel later strikes for Mindanao and move to the Visayas on the 12th. The task force moved in close and flew 2,400 sorties in two days; about 200 enemy planes were shot down or destroyed on the ground. Several ships were sunk and many installations destroyed.

It seemed to Halsey and his staff that the Japanese air forces were practically finished, and at noon on September 13, he sent a very important signal to Nimitz. He recommended that the Palau, Yap, Morotai, and Mindanao landings be cancelled as unnecessary, and that Task Force 38 and the men earmarked for these operations be diverted to MacArthur for an immediate seizure of Leyte. This signal was passed on to King and MacArthur.

With a force of fast carriers available MacArthur no longer needed to develop airfields in the southern Philippines before invading Leyte or Luzon; the Navy could furnish the air support the Army needed until it had captured or developed airfields on the target island.

If the 30,000 troops who were to land on Mindanao on November 15, and XXIV Corps (intended for Yap) could be diverted to Leyte, MacArthur would have an effective invasion force.

In MacArthur's name General Sutherland informed the J.C.S. and Nimitz on September 14 that if Halsey's recommendations were adopted, MacArthur would invade Leyte on October 20, that is two months ahead of the target date. Nimitz agreed, but said that the Palaus operation should not be cancelled because it would be needed as an anchorage and air base.

After their earlier performance, the J.C.S. acted with commendable alacrity. The Combined Chiefs-of-Staff conference, with Roosevelt, Churchill, and Mackenzie King, was still in session at Quebec when the new proposals came through. Breaking off from a dinner, the J.C.S. held a brief consultation. "Having the utmost confidence in General MacArthur, Admiral Nimitz and Admiral Halsey," wrote General Marshall, "It was not a difficult decision to make. Within 90 minutes after the signal

Pelileu airfield after it was taken by the 1st Marine Division.

had been received in Quebec, General MacArthur and Admiral Nimitz had received their instructions to execute the Leyte operation." The target date was fixed for October 20, and this avoided the three intermediate landings at Yap, the Talauds, and Mindanao. MacArthur's acknowledgment reached Marshall as he was leaving the dinner to return to his rooms.

The instructions were formalised soon after in the following message:

"1. Admiral Wilkinson's YAP ATTACK FORCE, the XXIV Army Corps, then loaded or at sea, will be assigned to General MacArthur to land LEYTE 20 October.

"2. All shipping used in the Palaus operation, after unloading, to be sent to Southwest Pacific ports to help VII 'Phib lift General Krueger's Sixth Army to LEYTE.

"3. ALL FIRE SUPPORT SHIPS and ESCORT CARRIERS used in the Palaus operation to be assigned temporarily to Admiral Kinkaid, Commander Seventh Fleet, to help cover LEYTE.

"4. ULITHI to be seized promptly, as an advanced fleet base".

There followed a series of planning conferences by the commanders of the forces involved. The operation would employ all the American military forces not engaged in Europe or on garrison duties in places like the Aleutian and Marshall Islands. Though no Australian troops were to be used, ships of the Royal Australian Navy would participate, and one ship of the Royal Navy, the fast minelayer Ariadne.

While the ships were assembled, and planning continued at all levels of command, the J.C.S. discussed the next move after Leyte. Was it to be Luzon, or Formosa?

After pressure against the Formosa operation by General Millard Harmon, commanding the Army Air Forces in the Central Pacific, and by General Simon Bolivar Buckner, commanding the 10th Army, it was shelved in favour of Luzon.

It was a logical and strategically sound move, for if Leyte could be captured in reasonable time, III and VII Amphibious Forces would be capable of putting in a second major landing before the end of 1944. Formosa would require an assault force of at least nine divisions, which would not be available until about the middle of 1945.

Japanese air strength was still too great to allow the invasion of Okinawa, so after clearing Luzon, the Americans could take Iwo

US Navy Fleet at anchor, Ulithi Lagoon, Caroline Islands, 6 Nov 1944.

Jima, as a rung in the "ladder up the Bonins", and Okinawa, as a base for air attacks and the final invasions of the Japanese home islands.

On October 3, 1944 the Joint Chiefs-of-Staff issued a directive to Nimitz and MacArthur, which seemed to be the final tribute to the general's skills as a salesman.

"General MacArthur will liberate Luzon, starting 20 December, and establish bases there to support later operations. Admiral Nimitz will provide fleet cover and support, occupy one or more positions in the Bonin-Volcano Island group 20 January 1945, and invade the Ryukyus, target date 1 March 1945."

Yet the liberation of the Philippines had been decided by

many events beyond his control. Landings on the China coast in support of the Formosa operation were ruled out because of the strength of the Japanese in both areas. Chinese Nationalist forces would be of little help, partly because of their lack of equipment and training, but also because of the enmity between Stilwell and Chiang Kai-shek.

The naval forces assigned to him from Halsey's Task Force 38, had been released through a misconception. Halsey believed that Japanese air-power in the Palaus, Mindanao, and Visayas was finished; in fact the Imperial General Headquarters had ordered that it be held back in readiness for the major landings which were expected in that area.

Yet despite this, the landings on Leyte and Luzon vindicated MacArthur's promise to return, and set the American forces in the Pacific on a return journey which would end less than 11 months after "Octagon", with the surrender of Japan.

Two amphibious operations brought the converging forces of MacArthur and Nimitz to within striking range of Leyte.

On September 15, 1944, the 31st Division under MacArthur began landing on Morotai island. He planned to expand its partially-completed airfield to cover operations to the south of the Philippine islands.

There was no opposition, but the airfield was unusable; another (ready for fighter operations on October 4 and bombers on the 15th) was quickly built.

On September 15 Halsey assaulted the Palau Islands. Fringed by coral reefs, this island group is 470 miles east of Mindanao. Halsey planned to use it as a seaplane base and anchorage for the attack on the Philippines.

The landing on Peleliu was strongly opposed. On the first day the 1st Marine Division had secured a beach-head; on the second it had occupied, but not secured, the airfield. The tough, well-sited bunkers which covered the airfield were eventually cleared, and by October 1 the field was taking fighters and a week later medium bombers. The Japanese, however, hung on in the island for another six weeks.

On September 17, the 81st Division landed on Angaur island, six miles south of Peleliu, and by noon had practically secured it. By the 21st an airstrip had been built and was taking Liberators. On the 23rd the 81st was landed on Ulithi atoll, which proved to be abandoned. It was quickly developed and became the main fleet base in October.

MacArthur, by way of the south-west, and Nimitz, through the central Pacific, had now reached their forming-up points for Leyte.

US Marine Corsair drops napalm on Japanese positions, Pelileu.

On the U.S. side, although everyone stuck to the item of the March 12 directive which laid down that the major objective of the coming offensive was to be Mindanao, opinion varied as to the direction the offensive was to take after this objective had been secured.

In the Pentagon Admiral King, supported, albeit with slight differences of opinion, by Nimitz, reckoned that there would be no harm in neglecting the rest of the Philippines and taking a leap forward to Formosa and Amoy on the south coast of China. This would cut communications between the Japanese homeland and its sources of raw materials and fuel, and would thus force a capitulation. But in his command post at Hollandia, General MacArthur was sickened by the idea of leaving Luzon and more than seven million Filipinos exposed to the rigours of a Japanese military occupation any longer. When he left Corregidor in March 1942, he had given his solemn promise to the Filipinos that he would return, and he did not intend that anyone should make him break his word. Roosevelt summoned MacArthur to Pearl Harbor and there MacArthur laid before him arguments not only of sentiment and prestige but also of sound military strategy:

"I argued against the naval concept of frontal assault against the strongly held island positions of Iwo Jima or Okinawa. In my argument, I stressed that our losses would be far too heavy to justify the benefits to be gained by seizing these outposts. They were not essential to the enemy's defeat, and by cutting them off from supplies, they could be easily reduced and their effectiveness completely neutralized with negligible loss to ourselves. They were not in themselves possessed of sufficient resources to act as main

Aerial view of US forces that invaded Leyte, Philippine Islands, 1944.

bases in our advance.

"In addition, I felt that Formosa, with a hostile population, might prove doubtful to serve as a base of attack against Japan itself."

This was how MacArthur, according to his memoirs, spoke to Roosevelt, who had Admiral Leahy with him. And, as it later turned out, MacArthur was to a certain extent right. He captured Luzon, at the cost of some 8,300 dead, between January 9 and June 25, 1945. The seven and a half square miles of the little island of Iwo Jima cost Nimitz 7,000 more, and Okinawa was captured by the U.S. 10th Army with the loss of 8,000 dead. As was his wont, the President took no part in this strategic debate, and Leahy and Nimitz were not insensitive to MacArthur's argument. The "Octagon" Conference, which opened at Quebec on September 11, 1944, envisaged, after preliminary operations and the capture of Mindanao, that there would be a landing at Leyte in the central Philippines on December 20, after which the two Allied forces in the Pacific would unite to occupy "either (1) Luzon to secure Manila by 2nd February, or (2) Formosa and Amoy on the China coast by 1st May 1945."

By now Nimitz's fleet was so large that it was decided to appoint two flag officers under him to command alternately. While one was at sea, the other would be at Pearl Harbor planning the next major operation. When commanded by Admiral Spruance it would be known as the 5th Fleet; while under Halsey, the 3rd Fleet. Sub-units would similarly exchange commanders and designations.

In August 1944 Spruance was relieved by Halsey, and Vice-Admiral Theodore Wilkinson relieved Richmond Turner in command of the 5th (now the 3rd) Amphibious Force. However, Mitscher remained in command of the Fast Carrier Force of 17 fast carriers, six new battleships, 13 cruisers, 58 destroyers, and 1,100 fighters, and dive- and torpedo-bombers, now Task Force 38 instead of 58.

On August 28, Halsey set out from Eniwetok to bombard Yap Island, the Palau Islands, and Mindanao, paving the way for the landings Nimitz and MacArthur were preparing at Peleliu and Morotai. The results exceeded all expectations: in 2,400 sorties Mitscher's squadrons shot down 200 enemy aircraft at a cost of only eight of their own and dealt a very hard blow to the Japanese

bases in this sector, giving MacArthur the necessary air superiority.

Leyte plans approved

Interpreting the weakness shown by the enemy somewhat optimistically, the impetuous Halsey submitted the following suggestion to Nimitz on September 13: cut out the intermediate objectives and make straight for Leyte. MacArthur seized upon this idea, remarking that this would save two months on the schedule and, as Nimitz agreed, the Chiefs-of-Staff, still in session at Quebec, took only an hour and a half to concur, such was the confidence of General Marshall and Admiral King in their subordinates. Yap and Mindanao were thus set aside and a landing on Leyte was fixed for October 20. On October 3, Allied commanders in the Central and South-West Pacific received the following directive for the next stage in the operations:

"General MacArthur will liberate Luzon, starting 20 December, and establish bases there to support later operations. Admiral Nimitz will provide fleet cover and support, occupy one or more positions in the Bonin-Volcano Island group 20 January 1945, and invade the Ryukyus, target date March 1945."

Formosa and Amoy were thus to be taken off the Pentagon's calendar of events. MacArthur and Nimitz, the one leaving from Australia and the other from Hawaii, were to meet in Leyte Gulf. Their commands remained contiguous, and the only transfer of units was that of 3rd Amphibious Force and XXIV Corps (Major-General J. R. Hodge) from Nimitz to MacArthur.

MacArthur takes Morotai …

Whilst waiting for the start of this new offensive operation, to be called "King II", MacArthur seized the island of Morotai north of Halmahera. His losses were insignificant as the Japanese were not expecting to be attacked. Yet its fall meant that the Moluccas were now useless to them.

… and Nimitz Peleliu

Meanwhile, Halsey's 3rd Fleet attacked Peleliu in strength. The island was defended by the excellent Japanese 14th Division, whose commander (Lieutenant-General Inouye) had intelligently applied the new instructions from Tokyo. Instead of the usual cordon of men defending the beach, he had deployed his forces in depth, taking advantage of the caves to provide cover from aerial and naval bombardment. And so, although the first wave of the U.S. 1st Marine Division (Major-General W. H. Rupertus) landed on September 15, it was not until November 25 that the last enemy surrendered, and meanwhile the Americans had had to bring in their 85th Division (Major-General P. J. Mueller) as reinforcement. The U.S. forces suffered considerable losses: 2,000 killed and over 8,500 wounded, or approximately the same as the garrison which they completely wiped out. On the other hand, in the same group of the Palau Islands, III Amphibious Force occupied the large atoll of Ulithi without loss, giving the U.S. 3rd Fleet a very safe, well-sited base 1,000 miles from Manila and 1,400 from Okinawa. This action ended on September 23.

So, ten months after the assault on Tarawa, Nimitz had reached a point 4,250 miles from Pearl Harbor.

"I have returned"

Between October 10 and 15, and using the method which had been so successful against the Gilberts, the Marshalls, and the Marianas, Task Force 38 ensured the success of Operation "King II" by plastering the bases on the Ryūkyū Islands, Formosa, and Luzon, from which the Japanese might have attacked the Leyte landings. A thousand Japanese planes took off, but Mitscher scored a clear victory, knocking out over 500 of them at a cost of 110 of his own. It is true that two cruisers were torpedoed during this action, which took Task Force 38 to within 60 miles of Formosa, but the U.S. Navy's rescue services were so efficient that the damaged ships were able to be towed to Ulithi. The Japanese airmen greatly exaggerated this little success, which was no compensation for the loss of their planes and some 40 merchant ships. They claimed to have sunk 11 aircraft-carriers, two battleships, and four cruisers and to have damaged or set on fire 28 other vessels. It would appear that the threat to the Japanese Empire had miraculously melted away.

This was what Tokyo was beginning to believe when, at dawn on October 17, a huge U.S. armada sailed into Leyte Gulf. It was the 7th Fleet under Vice-Admiral Thomas C. Kinkaid, 700 ships strong, which was also carrying 174,000 men of the U.S. 6th Army. On the same day, detachments seized the island commanding the entrance to Leyte Gulf then, for two whole days, the guns of the old battleships, cruisers, and destroyers of 3rd and 7th Amphibious Forces, or Task Forces 79 and 78, (Admirals T. S. Wilkinson and D. E. Barbey) roared out and the aircraft of 18

Macarthur wades ashore in the wake of the landings at Leyte, 1944.

escort carriers joined in.

The defence of the Philippines had been entrusted to the victor of Singapore, General Tomoyoki Yamashita, under Field-Marshal Count Hisaichi Terauchi, C.-in-C. Southern Army. Yamashita's 14th Area Army had seven divisions, with a total of 265,000 men, but on Leyte there was only one division, the 16th (Lieutenant-General Makino). However, the Japanese High Command had now decided to fight for Leyte rather than concentrate for the defence of Luzon, although the American attack had preempted their planned reinforcement.

The landing achieved local tactical surprise. In the evening of October 20 the U.S. 6th Army (General Krueger) had established a front of over 17 miles. On the right, X Corps (Major-General F. C. Sibert: 1st Cavalry and 24th Divisions) had occupied Tacloban and its aerodrome; on the left, XXIV Corps (Major-General J. R. Hodge: 96th and 7th Divisions) had got as far as Dulag, where 100,000 tons of material and stores had been landed on the beach. The cruiser Honolulu had been hit by an aerial torpedo, but this was the only noteworthy incident of the day. General MacArthur landed with the third wave: his promise to return had at last been kept. His implacable will and dynamic personality had ensured that the Philippines would have priority, but one major obstacle stood before his return to Manila: the remains of the Imperial Japanese fleet.

In expectation of the U.S. offensive, Admiral Toyoda, C.-in-C. Combined Fleet, had drawn up Plan "SHO GO" (Operation "Victory"), one variant of which was to cover the event which actually took place. And so at 0809 hours on October 17, he had merely to signal "SHO GO 1" from the Tokyo area for his subordinates to set the plan in motion.

Cunning though the plan was, it nevertheless meant 68 Japanese ships against 275 American, and a one to four inferiority in aircraft for the Japanese. Even including the planes they had in the Philippines, the Japanese were a long way from matching Halsey's and Kinkaid's 1,500. Also, it would take greater co-ordination than could be expected between Kurita and Nishimura to close their pincer in Leyte Gulf. Again, and this was the most important point, "SHO GO" envisaged nothing beyond October 25 and ignored what the 3rd Fleet was likely to do after Ozawa's diversion had fizzled out and Halsey set off full-steam ahead southwards with his 17 carriers and six fast battleships. If he did nothing, Toyoda would be left in Japan with Ozawa and no fuel oil, and Kurita would be left at Lingga with no ammunition or spare parts. Like Hitler on the Western Front, he was thus forced to go over to the offensive. He gave his order at 1100 hours on October 18.

Kurita mauled off Palawan ...

On October 22, having refuelled at Brunei, Kurita separated from Nishimura. At dawn on the 23rd he was heading north-east of the island of Palawan, a steppingstone between Borneo and Mindanao, when he was attacked by the submarines Dace and Darter (Commanders Claggett and McClintock). Dace scored a bulls-eye on the heavy cruiser Maya, which blew up. Darter scored a double, damaging the Takao so badly that she had to be sent back under escort, and sinking Kurita's flagship, the heavy cruiser Atago. The admiral was saved but he lost part of his signals and coding staff, which was to hamper his control of operations.

... and loses the giant battleship Musashi

Despite the loss of these three cruisers, Kurita was off Mindoro 24 hours later, and at the same time Nishimura was between Mindanao and Negros Islands. Shima, coming down from the north, was following Nishimura at a great distance and remained out of contact with him for fear of interception by U.S. tracking devices.

Ozawa finally set out from Kure on October 20 and progressed without incident along the path of sacrifice. In the evening of the 23rd the carrier Zuikaku, his flagship, sent out a long message designed to draw to herself the attentions of the enemy.

As expected, the Darter sent out a signal to report contact. This reached Halsey at 0620 hours on the 23rd. Nishimura and Shima were spotted in the early morning of the 24th. When he got McClintock's message from the Darter, the C.-in-C. of the 3rd Fleet, now reduced to Task Force 38, closed in to within 150 miles of the Philippines with his total force except for Vice-Admiral J. S. McCain's Task Group 38.1, which was re-forming at Ulithi. So Halsey had Rear-Admiral F. C. Sherman's Task Group 38.3 off Luzon, Rear-Admiral G. F. Bogan's Task Group 38.2 off San Bernardino Strait, and Rear-Admiral R. E. Davison Is Task Group

38.4 off Leyte. This gave Mitscher a total of 835 aircraft.

From the information given by tactical reconnaissance in the early morning of the 24th, Admiral Halsey deduced that he could leave all enemy forces observed in the south-east to be dealt with by Kinkaid and that he himself should concentrate his attention on the larger enemy force apparently intending to pass through the San Bernardino Strait. As one can never be too strong in attack, he ordered Vice-Admiral McCain to join him. Between 1026 and 1350 hours, Task Force 38 flew 259 sorties against Kurita's force, concentrating most of its attacks on the giant (64,200-ton) battleship Musashi. In spite of protective A.A. fire from nearly 130 guns, the Musashi was hit by 19 torpedoes and 17 bombs and went down during the evening with half her crew. The heavy cruiser Myoko had to be sent back to Brunei; three other cruisers suffered minor damage. These attacks forced the Japanese admiral to turn about and caused him to be late on the schedule agreed with Nishimura. No Japanese planes were used in this first engagement. Admiral Fukudome, C.-in-C. of the 2nd Air Fleet in the Philippines, considered that his pilots were incapable of measuring up to the U.S. airmen and sent them instead against 3rd Fleet. At the cost of heavy losses one of them scored a direct hit on the light carrier Princeton. Explosions and fires rent the unhappy vessel and caused heavy losses amongst the ships which went to her rescue. So Rear-Admiral Sherman ordered her to be finished off with a torpedo.

Japanese naval forces are brought into action by US Fleet, Leyte Gulf, 24 Oct 1944.

Halsey's controversial decision

Halsey now assumed that Kurita's force no longer offered a threat. He therefore took his entire fleet north to attack Ozawa's carriers, so completely taking the Japanese bait. His reaction has since been the subject of lively discussion in the U.S. Navy and Army. The day after his victory he explained his decision as follows:

"As it seemed childish to me to guard statically San Bernardino Strait, I concentrated TF 38 during the night and steamed north to attack the Northern Force at dawn. I believed that the Center Force had been so heavily damaged in the Sibuyan Sea that it could no longer be considered a serious menace to Seventh Fleet."

Nimitz's instructions

As we can see, Halsey greatly exaggerated the effects of his aircraft on Kurita's force, but he could not know that the hangars of the four enemy carriers, of whose approach he had just been informed, were half empty. He had to ask himself if his reconnaissance had given him the full tally of this new force. Moreover, by sailing northwards, Halsey was conscious of obeying the instructions of Nimitz who, as we have seen, required him to consider as his main mission the destruction of an important part of the Japanese fleet if the opportunity arose. This reveals the serious snags in the organisation of command as conceived by the Pentagon, for if the 3rd Fleet had been under MacArthur, there is no doubt that he would have forbidden it to leave the San Bernardino Strait uncovered.

Though he was told just before night-fall that Kurita had turned eastwards again, Halsey refused to part with his battleships, not wishing to leave them without air protection and wanting to give his carriers the cover of their guns. Mitscher, Bogan, and Vice-Admiral W. A. Lee, the last of whom commanded Task Force 34, all disapproved of their commander's initiative, but Halsey was in no mood to extemporise and they gave in.

Kinkaid destroys Nishimura and Shima

In Leyte Gulf, Vice-Admiral Kinkaid was hourly following the movements of Nishimura and Shima. He spent the afternoon setting a series of ambushes for them in Surigao Strait. He had six old battleships, eight cruisers, and 28 destroyers, whereas his adversary had only 19 warships altogether.

As Vice-Admiral Kinkaid sailed up the Surigao Strait between 2300 hours on October 24 and 0300 hours on the 25th, Nishimura was attacked by 30 P.T. boats, which fired torpedoes; all of them missed. A few minutes later his force, steaming in line ahead, was caught in a crossfire from the destroyers of the Eastern and Western Attack Groups under Captain Coward and Commander Phillips. The battleship Fuso was hit, and 30 minutes later broke in two; three destroyers were wrecked. Though hit, Nishimura's flagship, the battleship Yamashiro, maintained her course and, followed by the cruiser Mogami, sailed into Leyte Gulf. At 0353 hours Rear-Admiral G. L. Weyler's six battleships "crossed the T" and opened fire on the Japanese, loosing off 285 14- and 16-inch shells. Mogami succeeded in turning about, but Yamashiro capsized and sank at 0419 hours, taking down with her her obstinate admiral and almost all her crew. At this moment Shima appeared, having followed Nishimura some 30 miles behind. It did not take him long to sum up the situation, and at 0425 hours he decided on a "temporary withdrawal". In doing so he came under attack from the P.T. boats then, when dawn came, from the 7th Fleet's aircraft. All told, out of 19 Japanese ships which ventured into this trap, only two survived, including the old destroyer Shigure which had so often flirted with death in the Solomon Islands. Rear-Admiral J. B. Oldendorf lost 39 men killed and 114 wounded.

Kurita attacks again

On board their floating H.Q., the amphibious force flagship Wasatch, Kinkaid and his staff hardly had time to congratulate

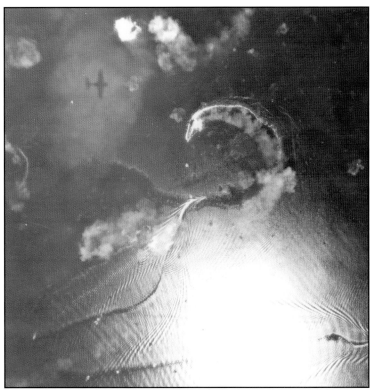

Japanese ships avoid aerial attack by US aircraft, Tables Strait, Leyte, 1944.

Kurita's force, much less heavily damaged than Halsey had supposed, had returned to the attack at the steady speed of 20 knots. Nishimura's catastrophe had in no way put Kurita off his intention of making for Leyte Gulf and destroying everything he found there.

At 0658 hours on October 25, the first shells fell on the American ships nearest the Japanese, Task Group 77.4.3 (Rear-Admiral Clifton A. F. Sprague).

If victory had depended on matériel superiority, the Americans would have suffered total defeat. No U.S. ship had a gun over 5-inch in calibre and the escort carriers' top speed was 20 knots. Kurita, on the other hand, had the 33 14-, 16-, and 18-inch guns of his four battleships, the 8- and 6.1-inch guns of his eight cruisers, and the torpedoes of his 15 destroyers. And the slowest of his ships could do five knots more than the fastest of the Americans'. But his first order was "General chase". This was a blunder, as it prevented any concerted action.

The Japanese fleet retires

This confusion allowed the Japanese no time to take advantage of their enormous numerical and matériel superiority. The carrier Gambier Bay was sunk by the 8-inch shells of the cruiser Chikuma which, together with her sister-ship Chokai, was then sunk by Commander R. L. Fowler's torpedo-bombers. The destroyer Johnston torpedoed the Kumano then, though hit by three 14-inch shells, went on fighting until the last of her guns was destroyed. The Hoel and the escort destroyer Samuel B. Roberts met with an equally heroic end. These sacrifices were not

themselves on their night victory at Surigao before the astounding news reached them that off Samar Island Task Group 77.4, consisting of 6 escort carriers and 20 destroyers under Rear-Admiral Thomas L. Sprague, was engaging a heavy Japanese force.

When asked by Kinkaid at 0412 hours "Is Task Force 34 guarding San Bernardino Strait?" Halsey had replied: "Negative. TF 34 is with carrier groups now engaging enemy carrier force."

Kinkaid had misinterpreted ambiguous instructions from Halsey which said that Task Force 34 "will be formed" to block the San Bernadino Strait — a statement of future intention, not of fact. Kinkaid was now exposed to attack by vastly more powerful forces.

in vain, as the heavy cruiser Suzuya was sunk in its turn. So E. B. Potter and Admiral Nimitz are right when they say of the battle off Samar:

"The history of the United States Navy records no more glorious two hours of resolution, sacrifice, and success."

Rear-Admiral C. A. Sprague writes: "At 0925 my mind was occupied with dodging torpedoes when near the bridge I heard one of the signalmen yell, 'Goddammit, boys, they're getting away!' I could not believe my eyes, but it looked as if the whole Japanese Fleet was indeed retiring. However, it took a whole series of reports from circling planes to convince me. And still I could not get the fact to soak into my battle-numbed brain. At best, I had expected to be swimming by this time."

All Kurita had to do at that moment was to draw in his forces so as to start again in better conditions, but on reflection he decided to pull out and before nightfall he had returned to the San Bernardino Strait. From the somewhat confused explanations of his decision he has given since the war, it turns out that he thought he was up against Task Force 38, and that he reckoned he had carried out his mission when his ships reported the destruction of three or four light carriers and several cruisers. The least that can be said is that he missed the chance of a great victory for which he would most likely have had to pay within the following 48 hours with an equally crushing defeat.

Kamikaze

Kurita's withdrawal did not put an end to the troubles of Task Group 77.4. Some hours later Vice-Admiral T. Ohnishi sent out his new weapon, the kamikazes. One of them sank the escort carrier Saint Lo, and five others caused losses and damage to five more. By the end of the day the battle off Samar had cost Thomas Kinkaid five ships, 23 planes, 1,130 men killed and 913 wounded.

Ozawa caught

At midnight on October 25, Admiral Ozawa had only 29 fighters and bombers left, whereas Halsey was bearing down on him with ten fast carriers, whose planes were to carry out 527 sorties in six waves from dawn to dusk. The first wave took off at 0540 hours. It caught the Japanese forces sailing north toward Halsey off Cape Engafio, sank the light carrier Chitose and left the fleet carrier Zuikaku so badly damaged that Ozawa had to transfer his flag to a cruiser. The second wave set fire to the light carrier Chiyoda, which was then left limping behind. Towards mid-day Mitscher sent up his third wave of 200 planes. This settled its account with the Zuikaku, the last survivor of the six carriers which had bombed Pearl Harbor. She succumbed under the blows of three torpedoes at 1414 hours. About an hour later, the fourth wave sank the light carrier Zutho.

Halsey and the pursuit

This success was only partial, however, as Halsey could not turn a deaf ear to Kinkaid's S.O.S., which came first in code then in clear. At 0848 he ordered McCain's task group to hasten to the rescue then, shortly before 1100 hours, on an orderfrom Nimitz, he sent Task Force 34 and Bogan's task group southwards. The Japanese withdrawal was greatly helped by these detachments,

Japanese aircraft carrier 'Yamato'.

though Rear-Admiral Du Bose's cruisers did finish off the Chiyoda with gunfire and sink two of Ozawa's destroyers. The latter also lost the light cruiser Tama, shattered by a clutch of torpedoes from the submarine Jallao.

Leyte Gulf, the greatest naval battle of all time, had involved 244 ships totalling 2,014,890 tons. By comparison, Jutland brought together under Scheer and Jellicoe some 254 ships totalling 1,616,836 tons. Thirty-two ships were lost.

Japan's impossible task

When questioned after the capitulation by an American commission of enquiry about the consequences of this battle, Admiral Yonai, Navy Minister in General Koiso's cabinet, replied:

"Our defeat at Leyte was tantamount to the loss of the Philippines. When you took the Philippines, that was the end of our resources."

Yamashita trapped in the Philippines

Indeed Yamashita was virtually cut off in the archipelago and, what is more, could only move his troops from one island to another with the greatest of difficulty, whereas his adversary had complete liberty of movement and almost unlimited supplies. In spite of a superiority of men and matériel, which increased in proportion to the Japanese losses, MacArthur never used overwhelming strength in hammer-blow attacks, but showed the same qualities as a tactician as he had done in the Papua agency.

If we realise that the reconquest of the Philippines required no fewer than 38 amphibious operations, we can see that no further comment is necessary unless it be to add to the praise of MacArthur a tribute to his airmen, Generals G. C. Kenney and E. C. Whitehead, and his sailors. Admirals T. C. Kinkaid and D. E. Barbey.

In the days following the landing on Leyte, nearly 50,000 Japanese still managed to get across to the island. The "no withdrawal" defence of Leyte fell to the Japanese 35th Army (Lieutenant-General Sasaku Suzuki). But its adversary, the U.S. 6th Army, increased from 101,000 men on November 12 to over 183,000 on December 2. MacArthur was cooking up one of his specials for Yamashita: on December 7 his 77th Division made a surprise landing in the Gulf of Ormoc on the west side of Leyte. Stabbed in the back, the 35th Army crumpled, then collapsed.

"I am exhausted. We have no food. The enemy are now within 500 meters from us. Mother, my dear wife and son, I am writing this letter to you by dim candle light. Our end is near. What will be the future of Japan if this island should fall into enemy hands? Our air force has not arrived. General Yamashita has not arrived. Hundreds of pale soldiers of Japan are awaiting our glorious end and nothing else. This is a repetition of what occurred in the Solomons, New Georgia, and other islands. How well are the people of Japan prepared to fight the decisive battle with the will to win … ?'

This was a last letter from a soldier of the Japanese 1st Division a few days before December 26, the end of the battle, when the Japanese had run out of men. 80,577 of them died, and 878 were taken prisoner. The U.S. 6th Army, with seven divisions, lost 3,508 killed and 12,076 wounded, two-thirds of these only lightly. On the same day it was relieved by the U.S. 8th Army.

MacArthur moves on

Without waiting to clear up on Leyte, MacArthur pressed on to Panay and Negros; then, when Yamashita had dropped his guard, Brigadier-General W. C. Dunckel's Western Visayan Task Force landed on Mindoro on December 15. This was 310 miles north of Leyte and it was taken without the loss of a single man. It brought U.S. aircraft to within striking distance of Luzon, the bay of Manila and Lingayen Gulf. The Philippines were now cut in two and Japanese communications with the Dutch East Indies were almost severed. Lingayen Gulf, from where the Japanese first landed on Luzon on December 22, 1941, was MacArthur's next objective. For this he gave I and XIV Corps (Major-Generals Innis W. Swift and Oscar W. Griswold respectively) to the 6th Army. The divisions involved were the 6th and 43rd (I Corps) and 37th and 41st (XIV Corps). Transport and supplies were to be the job of III and VII Amphibious Forces.

After a decoy action to make Yamashita think that the invasion of Luzon would come from Mindoro, the Americans landed on January 9, 1945, and met no stronger opposition than some sporadic mortar fire. A week later they were 30 miles along the road to Manila for the loss of 900 men, including 250 killed.

In the restricted waters off-shore the kamikaze corps, under Vice-Admiral Takijiro Ohnishi, had some success against the U.S. 7th Fleet. In the Mindoro operation on December 15 one of them damaged the cruiser Nashville, causing her to turn back with 131 dead and 158 wounded on board, including Vice-Admiral A. D. Struble. During the Lingayen landings between January 1 and 31, 54 U.S. and Australian ships were attacked by these suicide planes but, apart from the escort carrier Ommaney Bay and two small ships, they all survived. On January 6, however, on the bridge of the battleship New Mexico, Lieutenant-General Sir Herbert Lumsden, British liaison officer with MacArthur, was killed, giving the Anglo-Saxons a foretaste of what they were to get off Okinawa.

Japanese carrier under attack off Cape Engano, Leyte Gulf, 25 Oct 1944.

The first Americans to return to the Philippines were a small Ranger task force with their destroyer transports and escort.

The Dinagat Attack Group, under Rear-Admiral Arthur D. Struble, transported the 500 men of Company D, 6th Ranger Battalion, U.S. Army, commanded by Lieutenant-Colonel H. A. Mucci. In the darkness of October 17 and 18, 1944 they were to demolish the Japanese radio location equipment on four islands at the two entrances to Leyte Gulf. If these electronic feelers were not ripped out, it was feared that they would signal the arrival of the invasion fleet on the 20th.

The main landings were planned for mid-day to allow a daylight run into the gulf, in which floating mines and obstacles had been reported. Throughout the morning the warships moved into position, and the transports halted about eight miles off the beach. The landing craft were hoisted out, and began circling round their larger parent ships. The noise and apparent confusion of a major amphibious operation had begun to build up.

From 0700, fire support units had been in action in the pre-landing shoot. First to arrive were the battleships Mississippi, Maryland, and West Virginia. At 0900 they were relieved by the Close Covering Group, after they had sent 30 shells per main battery gun rumbling over the fleet into the jungle coast line.

Throughout these manoeuvres, fighters, torpedo-bombers, and reconnaissance aircraft from the 3rd and 7th Fleets made attacks on the airfields in northern Mindanao, Cebu, Negros, Panay, and Leyte, and conducted sweeps over the surrounding areas.

Rear-Admiral D. E. Barbey, whose air plan was administered by Captain Whitehead, had ordered a break in the bombing and strafing of the beach 45 minutes before H-hour. This was a departure from the standard operating procedure of that time. The gap was covered by high-angled naval gunfire and rocket barrages from 0915 to 1000.

By 0930 the bombardment was reaching its cacophonous climax and the landing craft had formed up for the 5,000 yard dash for the beach. At 0943 the signal flag was run up on the control vessel PC-623, and preceded by 11 L.C.I. rocket craft, the boats went in.

In a couple of minutes the L.C.I.s had fired 10,000 4.5-inch rockets in a close pattern over the northern and southern landing areas.

Behind the L. C.I.s came the first wave of amphtrack tanks, followed by L.V.T.s and then the amphtrack personnel carriers. By the time the fourth wave had hit

"Red" Beach in the northern landing area, the enemy had begun to hit back with mortars sited in the neighbouring hills. With the correct range and deflection they dropped bombs on the L.C.V.(P.)s from the Elmore and sank a boat from Aquarius, killing 3 men and injuring 15.

On the southern beaches a 75-mm battery near Catmon Hill took on the destroyer Bennion, straddling her repeatedly and wounding five men with a near miss. Artillery and mortar fire fell on "Blue" Beach as the 96th Division was landing.

Both the Japanese and the Americans realised that they had begun a battle that was of considerable strategic importance. If the Japanese lost the Philippines they would no longer control the sea-lanes to the oil of the Netherlands East Indies, tin and rubber from Malaya, and rice from Indo-China, nor have access to the varied mineral resources of the islands themselves.

The American leaders Roosevelt, Nimitz, and the Joint Chiefs-of-Staff had been persuaded by General MacArthur, and also by the course of the war, that the capture of the Philippines would be easier than that of Formosa, and would liberate a large and loyal population.

It would also cut off supplies to Japan and give the Americans a base for operations leading to the invasion of the Japanese home islands.

Yamashita's threadbare forces

With this in mind, each adversary approached the battle with as much determination and as many resources as he could muster.

Field-Marshal Terauchi (Southern Army) whose area included the Philippines, had made the 14th Area Army and the 4th Air Army responsible for their defence. The 14th Army was so under strength that he had ordered it to concentrate on the defence of Luzon and regard the southern islands as of secondary importance.

The 14th Army consisted of eight infantry divisions and three independent mixed brigades. On October 6, Lieutenant-General T. Yamashita, the "Tiger of Malaya", had assumed command. He made Lieutenant-General S. Suzuki, with three infantry divisions and two mixed brigades, responsible for the defence of the central and southern islands. Suzuki in turn gave the 16th Division, under Lieutenant-General S. Makino, the task of defending Leyte.

The island which Makino had to defend is about 115 miles

A Water tank trap laid by the Japanese to hamper US invasion.

long north to south, and between 15 and 45 miles wide east to west. It is rugged and mountainous, except for a strip of flat land running north from Ormoc in the west, and a broad fertile valley in the north-east which narrows and fades out halfway down the east coast. The main Japanese airstrips were one each at Tacloban near the entrance to the San Juanico Strait and at Dulag 11 miles to the south, with three at Burauen further inland. It was on two beaches near Tacloban and Dulag that MacArthur planned to land.

He was assembling his invasion forces at Hollandia, which had become the main base in New Guinea, and at Manus in the Admiralty Islands. Naval forces consisted of the U.S. 7th Fleet

(Vice-Admiral T. C. Kinkaid), which included two cruisers and two destroyers from the Royal Australian Navy, and the Ariadne, a fast minelayer of the Royal Navy. The U.S. 3rd Amphibious Force had joined it from the central Pacific. The U.S. 3rd Fleet, under Halsey, which included four fast carrier groups, was to cover and support MacArthur, but would remain under Nimitz's orders. The U.S. 6th Army (X and XXIV Corps), under Lieutenant-General W. Krueger, provided the land forces and the 5th U.S.A.A.F. the supporting air force.

Carrier strikes

In preparation for the landings, the 15 fast carriers of the 3rd Fleet made a series of heavy raids on Japanese bases in Okinawa, Luzon, and Formosa. They came under very heavy aerial attack during these operations and between October 10 and 17 lost 26 aircraft and had two cruisers put out of action.

The Japanese, however, claimed that they had sunk two battleships and 11 carriers, and damaged many others, for the loss of 320 aircraft. Basing their moves on these spurious successes they altered their plans for the defence of Leyte and the Philippines.

Admiral S. Toyoda, Commander-in-Chief of the Japanese Combined Fleet, ordered the land-based aircraft to undertake the decisive battle for the Philippines under the operational title "SHO-1". The 2nd Air Fleet (350 operational aircraft) together with 150 carrier aircraft of Vice-Admiral J. Ozawa's 3rd and 4th Carrier Divisions, moved to Formosa. The 5th Fleet (Vice-Admiral K. Shima), consisting of the 16th and 21st Cruiser

US troops use 60mm mortar to shell Japanese pillboxes.

Squadrons, was ordered to sail from the Inland Sea to seek out and destroy any American ships damaged in the action.

5th fleet moves on

Concurrently with these moves the Imperial General Headquarters instructed Southern Army to fight the decisive battle on Leyte instead of Luzon. Terauchi ordered the 14th Area Army to deploy its maximum strength to hold the island. Yamashita protested, but the order was repeated on the 22nd, two days after the American landings, and so he ordered the 35th Army to concentrate for the defence of Leyte.

The naval section of Imperial General Headquarters

subsequently discovered that the reports of U.S. naval losses were inaccurate, and ordered the 5th Fleet to make for the Ryukyu islands. This information, however, was not passed on to Yamashita. The land forces were now committed to Leyte without naval support.

MacArthur's powerful forces

For the Leyte invasion MacArthur had 200,000 men of General Walter Krueger's 6th Army, Lieutenant-General C. Kenney's 2,500 combat aircraft, and the 7th Fleet-often called "MacArthur's Navy" which had an additional 500 aircraft. The 3rd Fleet had 1,000 aircraft as well as nearly 100 of the most modern warships in the world.

He would need these resources because the invasion would be conducted out of range of land-based aircraft. However, MacArthur did not exercise direct command over Halsey and the 3rd Fleet, who were under Nimitz and so could be ordered away to attack the Japanese fleet if it approached.

Airstrips: the vital factor

The 7th Fleet had some small escort carriers, but they would be inadequate to defend the fleet and transports, and cover the beach-head if major units of the Japanese Navy or Air Forces succeeded in evading the 3rd Fleet. Consequently it was essential that Kenney's Far East Air Forces should start operating from local airstrips as soon as the invasion forces had captured them.

With this in mind the invasion beaches chosen were close to, or opposite, the coastal airstrips near Tacloban and Dulag.

As soon as he heard of the landings, Suzuki (35th Army) instructed the 16th Division to keep control of the airfields at all costs, and ordered Leyte to be reinforced by four battalions. On the October 22 Yamashita told him that he was to fight a decisive battle on Leyte and that he would be getting two divisions and an independent mixed brigade from Luzon. With further reinforcements from Davao and Cebu, Suzuki had the equivalent of four strong divisions on the island.

If the decisive naval and air battles were successful, the Japanese land forces could be sent against the estimated two divisions which the Americans had put ashore. The 16th Division was ordered to hold a line Burauen–Dagami, whilst the bulk of the Japanese forces concentrated in the Carigara plain.

These deployments assisted the Americans, who advanced rapidly against light opposition, and by November 2 the 6th Army had reached a line Carigara–Jaro–Dagami–Abuyog. They had an advanced detachment at Baybay and had captured all five airstrips.

"I have returned"

Before examining the American plans for the break-out from their beach-head, let us recall an incident which took place on the first day.

General George MacArthur had last visited Leyte Gulf in 1903 as a 2nd Lieutenant of Army Engineers. Forty-one years later he boarded a landing craft with President Osmeña, Resident Commissioner Romulo, Chief-of-Staff Sutherland, and Air Commander Kenney.

Japanese destroyer is broken in two, after repeated attacks by US aircraft.

After the craft had grounded, MacArthur waded through the knee-deep surf, inspected the beach, and walked inland about 200 yards to examine the effects of the bombardment.

It may not have looked like the return of a conquering hero, but MacArthur made up for this in his broadcast on the "Voice of Freedom" network.

Standing on the beach in front of the microphone, his hands shook and his voice betrayed his deep emotion:

"People of the Philippines, I have returned. By the grace of Almighty God our forces stand again on Philippine soil."

He urged the population to rally to him, and also introduced the new president Sergio Osmeña. A passionate yet restrained speech, it was an outlet for powerful emotions held in check and only betrayed earlier when, with a smile, he had remarked "Well, believe it or not, we're here."

After the war General Yamashita said that he had imagined that the film of MacArthur's return had been mocked up in New Guinea. Had he known that the general was at the front he would have launched the whole strength of the Japanese forces in a suicide raid on MacArthur's headquarters to avenge the death of Admiral Yamamoto.

Meanwhile unloading was proceeding at a fast and sometimes chaotic rate. L.S.T.s originally intended for "Red" Beach were diverted to Tacloban air- strip, and here the rapidly-growing supply dump began to restrict the work of the airfield engineers.

On October 24, Kenney made the drastic threat that everything not removed from the airstrip by dawn on the 25th would be bulldozed.

Japanese reinforcements

Between October 22 and December 11, the Japanese succeeded in reinforcing the original garrison of 15,000 men with some 45,000 men and 10,000 tons of stores. Their operations cost them one light cruiser, eight destroyers, six escort craft, and 17 transports-shipping they could ill afford to lose. Despite this, the 35th Army was outnumbered by the 6th Army, whose strength stood at 183,000 by December 2.

By November 1, Suzuki realised that he was up against two American corps, each of two divisions, and that he lacked the strength to carry out his original plan. He ordered the 1st Division and the truncated 26th, when they arrived at Carigara and Jaro respectively, to hold the U.S. X Corps in the north. The remaining reinforcements were sent to assist the 16th Division under attack by the U.S. XXIV Corps in the south. In the ensuing heavy fighting the Americans were halted near Limon and to the west of Jaro.

At a conference with Terauchi, on November 9 and 10, Yamashita urged that the reinforcement of Leyte was weakening the defences of Luzon, and proving too costly in transports and naval vessels. Terauchi agreed that there was little hope of holding the island and that supply operations should cease.

Yamashita plans …

Despite this, Yamashita ordered the 35th Army to use the 26th Division on the Burauen front with a view to launching an attack with the 16th Division to recapture some of the airfields. Suzuki, who had hoped to concentrate his forces in the north, was now forced to send the 26th Division along the Albuera–Burauen track and the 102nd Division to the Mount Pina area to protect the right of the 1st Division, holding out at Limon. The 4th Air Army proposed an air borne counter-attack with the 40 aircraft and 250 paratroops of the 2nd Raiding Group, which had flown in from Japan. Yamashita decided that a joint air and ground attack should be launched near the end of the month, preceded by an air attack between the 23rd and 27th.

… the counter-attack

In a spectacular, but fumbled, attack on November 27, three transport aircraft carrying demolition troops were sent to crash-land on the strips at Dulag and Tacloban.

One aircraft crashed on Buri airstrip killing all its occupants, the second hit the beach and most of the men escaped, and the third landed in the surf near the H.Q. of the U.S. 728th Amphibious Battalion, between Rizal and Tarragona. A brisk hand-to-hand fight ensued, in which some Japanese were killed and others escaped to the jungle.

A second and more serious attempt was made on the Buri strip on the night of December 5–6. About 150 infantrymen had worked down through the mountains and attacked American troops bivouacking near the strip. The Japanese were driven off at dawn.

Paratroop landings fail

Through a piece of bad co-ordination, the paratroop attack came 20 hours later. Between 39 and 40 aircraft, carrying about 15 to 20 men apiece, roared over Tacloban and Dulag. At the former they were destroyed or driven off by the A.A. fire, while the Dulag section crash-landed killing crew and paratroopers.

However, a drop from 35 different aircraft on the Burauen strips met with greater success. The Japanese set fire to stores, fuel, ammunition, and some small liaison aircraft. For two days and nights ground crews and other air force personnel stalked one another and the Japanese, before the paratroopers were eliminated.

Ironically, the weather had proved more effective than these airborne sorties, for the U.S.A.A.F. had abandoned the Burauen strips, which had become waterlogged, leaving only rear echelon units behind.

With his X Corps held up near Limon, and XXIV Corps delayed in its advance north from Baybay, Krueger decided to make a fresh landing south of Ormoc, to drive a wedge between the two wings of his opponents.

On the morning of the 7th, the U.S. 77th Division landed four miles south of Ormoc and met no resistance. The convoy and escorts, however, came under attack after the landing and during the return, and lost two destroyers sunk and two damaged to kamikaze attacks.

Suzuki was forced to switch his 16th and 26th Divisions from the front to oppose this landing. On December 10, however, the 77th beat him in the race for Ormoc.

With the main Japanese base in American hands, Yamashita told Suzuki that he was on his own. Japanese resistance began to crumble fast. On December 20, X Corps and the 77th Division met at Cananga, and part of this force turned west. On Christmas Day, with the help of a force moved by sea from Ormoc, it captured Palompon, the only port of any significance left to the Japanese.

Though organised resistance ceased, there were still groups of Japanese obeying Yamashita's order to live off the country and keep up the struggle with the Americans. As the official naval history comments "Japanese unorganised resistance can be very tough." Following his instructions to keep up the struggle, Yamashita added a message explaining that the high command had decided to concentrate on the defence of Luzon, and that he was shedding "tears of remorse" for the tens of thousands of his countrymen who must fight to the death on Leyte.

Mopping up continued until March 17, 1945. There was still over a full division of Japanese troops on the island. Some used the rugged and badly-mapped terrain for guerrilla tactics, whilst small units tried to escape to Cebu across the 25 miles of the Camotes Sea.

By March 1945, despite sweeps by the U.S. 77th Division, there were still several thousand Japanese at large. On March 17, two ships appeared off the coast and embarked Suzuki and part of his staff. For a month they sailed in search of a Japanese-held port until on April 16 they were caught by U.S. aircraft off Negros, and General Suzuki was killed.

Small groups of Japanese continued to be hunted and killed by Filipino guerrillas until the end of the war.

The Leyte campaign was a costly operation. The U.S. Navy and Marine Corps lost several hundred men on and around the island, in addition to the heavy losses sustained in the battle off Samar.

The Army, not including the A.A.F., had 15,584 battle casualties, of which the 3,508 killed were about equally distributed between X and XXIV Corps. In January their full strength stood at 257,766 officers and men.

Understandably, estimates of Japanese casualties vary greatly. The 6th and 8th Armies reported 80,557 confirmed dead, almost one-third of which had occurred during the mopping up operations. The American forces took only 828 Japanese prisoners.

Mobile 8-inch howitzers on Leyte.

Despite the fact that Luzon, the "capital island" of the Philippines, was the largest Japanese-held island between New Guinea and Tokyo, the American planners had by no means been unanimous in the opinion that it should be recaptured. Admirals King and Nimitz had argued that it would be better, once a foothold had been established in the Philippines with the capture of Leyte and Mindanao, to bypass Luzon and go straight for Formosa. General MacArthur was the passionate champion of the liberation of all the Philippine islands before making the next advance towards Japan. When it was decided to invade Leyte in October 1944 — two months ahead of the original schedule — MacArthur announced that he would be ready to invade Luzon by the end of December, giving the 20th as a provisional date. This was so much in advance of the earliest possible date by which an invasion force could be deployed for an assault on Formosa that it was decided -a fortnight before the troops went in on Leyte-to invade Luzon.

MacArthur was forced to postpone the date for the Luzon landing by the slow progress of the battle for Leyte. Here the American forces were bedevilled by sluicing autumnal rains, which converted the island battlefield into a quagmire. By the end of November the Luzon attack had been put back to the second week of January: the 9th. In addition, it was decided to capture the island of Mindoro as a curtain-raiser to the main landing on Luzon. This would mean that the Luzon force would not have to rely on the flooded airfields on Leyte — apart from the fleet aircraft-carriers — to provide air cover for the landings. Mindoro, right on Luzon's doorstep, would provide excellent "frontline"

airstrips for round-the-clock operations; and its capture was entrusted to a specially-formed unit known as the Western Visayan Task Force. Consisting of two reinforced regiments under the command of Brigadier-General William C. Dunckel, it was to attack on December 15, while the struggle for Leyte was still moving to its close.

During the three-day voyage from Leyte to Mindoro the ships of the Task Force had to endure heavy kamikaze attacks; the flagship Nashville was badly damaged by a kamikaze, and Dunckel himself was wounded (though he was able to stay in command). But the Mindoro landing went in according to plan on the morning of the 15th. It was unopposed; Dunckel's men pegged out a large beach-head with no difficulty and work on the airstrips began at once, while the interior was still being mopped up. By December 23 two new airstrips were already in use on Mindoro and the build-up of aircraft for the Luzon attack could begin. To use MacArthur's own words, "Mindoro was the gate": the turn of Luzon had come.

Yamashita's problems

On paper, the Japanese force which would defend Luzon looked a formidable one: over 250,000 men of the 14th Area Army, commanded by General Tomoyuki Yamashita. But in fact Yamashita's prospects were not bright, and he knew it very well. Most of his units were under-strength and short of supplies. The virtual elimination of the Japanese Combined Fleet at Leyte Gulf meant that he would be getting no more supplies by sea. And the air battles during the prolonged fight for Leyte had whittled down

South East Luzon, retarded bombs fall on camouflaged Japanese convoy.

Fleet. The 7th Fleet — over 850 vessels strong — included the battle fleet, under Vice-Admiral Jessie B. Oldendorf, which had smashed Nishimura's battle squadron in the Surigao Strait during the battle of Leyte Gulf, and which was now to spearhead the invasion of Luzon by bombarding the landing beaches. Admiral William F. Halsey's 3rd Fleet would provide strategic air cover by launching carrier strikes on northern Luzon and Formosa, and land-based air cover would be the contribution of General George F. Kenney's Far East Air Forces, which would begin the battle from their bases on Leyte and Mindoro.

Bombardment and assault

It was obvious to both sides where the invasion must be directed: across the superb beaches of Lingayen Gulf, which was where the Japanese had landed their main forces in December 1941. Lingayen Gulf leads directly into the central plain of Luzon, to Manila and the magnificent anchorage of Manila Bay.

Yamashita was not going to attempt to meet the invaders on the beaches, nor offer them a set-piece battle once ashore. He grouped his forces in three major concentrations which, he hoped, would confine the Americans to the central plain. Yamashita's strategy, in short, was very like Rommel's attempts to "rope off" the Allies in the Normandy bocage after D-Day. But — as events in Normandy had already proved conclusively — the most dogged defence was not likely to hold out for long against an invader with control of the air and uninterrupted supplies and reinforcements from the sea.

On January 2, 1945, the first ships of Oldendorf's

the number of operational aircraft on Luzon to around 150. These would have no chance of halting the American invasion force as it approached Luzon, let alone of commanding the skies over the land battlefield. Yamashita knew that his troops would not be able to stop the invaders getting ashore, and that he did not have sufficient men to defend the whole of Luzon.

In total contrast was the strength of the American forces. They were organised in the fashion which had launched the attack on Leyte. The land fighting was entrusted to General Walter Krueger's 6th Army — over 200,000 men, exclusive of reinforcements — which would be conveyed to its destination and shielded on landing by Vice-Admiral Thomas C. Kinkaid's 7th bombardment force headed out of Leyte Gulf, their destination Lingayen. A punishing ordeal lay ahead of them, for they became the prime targets for Luzonbased kamikaze attacks which began on the 4th, while Oldendorf's force was still threading its way through the Sulu Sea. On that day a twin-engined kamikaze crashed into the escort carrier Ommaney Bay, damaging her so badly that she was beyond salvation and had to be sunk. On the 5th the American force was well within reach of the Japanese airfields on Luzon — under 150 miles — and the kamikaze attacks rose in pitch. In the afternoon, while the Americans were passing the mouth of Manila Bay, 16 kamikazes broke through the American air screen and attacked, inflicting damage on nearly a dozen American and Australian ships, including two escort carriers, two heavy cruisers, and two destroyers. Nor were the Japanese attacks confined to aircraft alone; two Japanese destroyers appeared, but were seen off in short order. Air strikes from the escort carriers sank one, Momi, and damaged the other.

On January 6 Oldendorf's ships entered Lingayen Gulf and began to move into position for the bombardment — and the kamikaze attacks reached their climax. The weather was working for the Japanese. A low, dense overcast blanketed the airfields on northern Luzon, preventing Halsey's pilots from masking them with continuous patrols. Bad weather meant nothing to the Japanese pilots — except that their chances of immolating themselves on their targets were enhanced. By nightfall on the 7th two American battleships — New Mexico and California — three cruisers, three destroyers, and several other vessels had been more or less badly damaged, and three of them, fast minesweepers

(Palmer, Long, and Hovey), sunk. But this was the last great effort of the kamikazes of Luzon. On the 7th, Halsey's planes battered the Luzon airfields so heavily that the last operational Japanese aircraft were withdrawn from the Philippines.

Oldendorf's ships had played an invaluable rôle in soaking up the punishment which might otherwise have savaged the troop transports' and landing-craft bringing the invasion force. Now they went ahead with their bombardment programme, which raged for the next three days. Early on the morning of January 9 the troop convoys moved into Lingayen Gulf. At 0700 hours the final stage of the pre-landing barrage was opened and at 0900 the first wave of landing-craft headed in to the beaches. Shortly after 0930 the spearhead troops were ashore-but there were no Japanese troops to meet them. Yamashita had pulled back all his forces not only from the beaches but from the immediate hinterland, with the result that by nightfall on the 9th Krueger's army had established for itself a beach-head 17 miles wide, which reached four miles inland at its deepest extremities. And, true to form, MacArthur himself had landed in triumph, duly captured for posterity by the camera.

The 6th Army punch was a two-corps affair. On the right flank was Major-General Oscar W. Griswold with XIV Corps, consisting of the 37th and 40th Infantry Divisions. Griswold's corps had the task of breaking through to Manila and liberating the capital, a task obviously dear to MacArthur's heart. But before this could be done the, left flank of the lodgment area had to be made secure from any heavy counter-attacks from the north, and this was the job of Major-General Innis P. Swift's I Corps (the 6th and 43rd Infantry Divisions). Until Swift had made the left flank secure, Krueger was going to take his time about pushing on to Manila-and he was wise to do so. For Swift's corps was faced by the "Shobu" Group, the largest of Yamashita's three concentrations, 152,000-men strong and well dug in along a chain of strongpoints 25 miles long, from Lingayen Gulf to the Cabaruan Hills. Foul weather on the 10th, ramming home the vulnerability of the landing beaches by causing considerable disruption, made it clear that Swift's task was of vital importance. But his progress against the tough Japanese defences remained slow, much to MacArthur's chagrin. Not until the end of the month did I Corps, reinforced with the 25th and 32nd Divisions, push the Japanese back into the mountains after a tank battle at San Manuel on the 28th. They reached the approaches to Yamashita's H.Q. at Baguio and drove east through San Jose to reach the eastern shore of Luzon, pushing a corridor across the island. This now cut off Yamashita from his troops in the island's centre and south.

Griswold and XIV Corps met with scanty opposition as they began their advance to the south. By the 16th they were across the Agno river, still with little or no opposition — but Krueger was yet unwilling to push too far ahead in the south until he was convinced that the northern flank was secure. But on January 17 MacArthur intervened, stressing the need for an immediate drive on Manila. There were plenty of good reasons. The Americans needed the port; they needed the airfield complex at Clark Field for Kenney's planes; and they were anxious to liberate the inmates of military and civilian prison camps before the Japanese had time

to harm them further. But now Griswold's corps in its turn came up against the second of Yamashita's defensive concentrations. d The flamboyant General MacArthur took every opportunity to visit the troops in the front line and boost their morale. Here troops aboard the Nashville crowd the decks as he embarks in a landing craft to visit his men ashore.

Battle for Manila

The second part of Yamashita's forces that the American troops encountered on Luzon was the "Kembu" Group, 30,000 men under Major-General Rikichi Tsukada, stationed in the mountains west of the central plain of Luzon to defend the Clark Field sector. Griswold's corps first encountered heavy opposition from the "Kembu" Group at the town of Bamban on January 23. It took over a week of extremely heavy fighting before XIV Corps forced the Japanese back from Clark Field. By January 31 the "Kembu" Group had lost over 2,500 men and had been forced to retreat into the mountains; the Clark Field complex was in American hands and Griswold was able to resume his drive on Manila.

In the last days of January, two more American units landed on Luzon. The first was XI Corps, commanded by Major-General Charles P. Hall, consisting of the 38th Infantry Division and a regiment of the 24th Division. It landed on the west coast of the island to the north of the Bataan Peninsula, and its mission was to capture the Olongapo naval base and drive across the root of the Bataan Peninsula to Manila Bay. Unlike MacArthur in 1942, Yamashita refused to run the risk of getting any of his troops trapped on Bataan, but Hall's corps had two weeks of tough fighting before it reached Manila Bay. The second landing went in south of the bay at Nasugbu, 50 miles south-west of Manila. It was made by the bulk of the 11th Airborne Division; the plan was to tie down Japanese troops in southern Luzon and open up a second approach route to the capital. On February 3 the rest of the division dropped inland, on Tagaytay Ridge; the division concentrated and moved north-east towards Manila, but was stopped on the outskirts.

It was clear that if Manila was to be taken it would have to be from the north. Once again the impetus came from MacArthur. "Go to Manila!" he urged on January 30. "Go around the Nips, bounce off the Nips, but go to Manila!" His exhortations went right down the line of Griswold's corps to the two divisions which would do the job: the 37th Infantry and the newly-arrived 1st Cavalry.

Their main concern and objective was the big civilian internment camp at Santo Tomas, which was liberated on February 3 by a "flying column" of tanks from the 1st Cavalry. The prisoners in Santo Tomas were in an unenviable position, hearing the sounds of a tough battle outside the walls and fearing the worst until an unmistakable American bellow of "Where the hell's the front gate?" was followed by 1st Cavalry tanks smashing through the entrance. Hard on the heels of 1st Cavalry came the 37th Infantry, which pushed through to Old Bilibid Prison and liberated 1,300 civilian internees and P.O.W.s. The northern suburbs of Manila were in American hands. But the battle for the city was only beginning.

In 1942 MacArthur had declared Manila an open city rather than turn it into a battlefield, and Yamashita had no intention of fighting for the city in 1945. But there were 17,000 fighting men in Manila over whom he had no control — they were not Army troops. They were naval forces under the command of Rear-Admiral Sanji Iwabachi, who was determined to hold Manila to the last. He split his men into separate battle groups, gave each of them a section of the city to defend, and prepared for an all-out battle. A unique episode was about to be added to the history of the Pacific war: its only urban battle.

The Americans took sometime to realise what lay before them, but a week of vicious fighting and' rapidly-mounting casualties forced them, to accept that there could be no question of taking Manila without cracking the Japanese out of their positions at the expense of the city's buildings. By the 12th, XIV Corps had forced the Japanese in front of them back into Intramuros, the old walled inner city of Manila. South of the city the paratroopers of the 11th Airborne Division had run up against tough defensive positions built by the Japanese sailors on Nichols Field. Here, too, an inch-by-inch struggle developed, with the paratroopers getting artillery support from the guns of XIV Corps to the north. It was an unrelieved killing-match, eliciting a grim signal from one of 11th Airborne's company commanders: "Tell Halsey to stop looking for the Jap Fleet; it's dying on Nichols Field."

Even after the 11th Airborne joined hands with 1st Cavalry on February 12, the battle for Manila was far from over. Iwabachi's sailors held on grimly both in Intramuros and the rest of the city and over a fortnight of murderous fighting lay ahead. It was given a fresh element of horror by the fact that the Japanese refused to evacuate non-combatants, and it went on until the very last flickers of Japanese resistance were stamped out on March 3. MacArthur's obsession with the recapture of Manila had exacted a terrible price. The Filipino capital lay in ruins. Civilian casualties have been set as high as 100,000. American losses topped 1,000 killed and 5,500 wounded. As for the Japanese defenders of Manila, they had upheld the fighting traditions of the Imperial Japanese Navy by dying virtually to a man.

While the slaughter in Manila was still running its course, the clearing of the island forts in Manila Bay had begun. First came the overrunning of the Bataan Peninsula by XI Corps, begun on the 14th and aided by a landing at Mariveles, at the tip of the peninsula, on the following day. It only took a week to flush the scanty Japanese forces out of their positions on Bataan; compared with the carnage in Manila it was an easy task.

Corregidor, the strongest fortress in Manila Bay, was a different story. In May 1942 the American garrison had capitulated within 48 hours of the first Japanese landings on the island. In 1945 it took over ten days of bitter fighting before the Americans got the island back. Their assault went in, on February 16, a combined parachute drop and amphibious landing which rapidly gained control of the surface defences'. But the Japanese still had to be flushed from their positions underground, and the island was not declared secure until the 28th. MacArthur himself visited Corregidor on March 2. Ready as always with a memorable bon mot, he announced: "I see that the old flagpole still stands. Have your troops hoist the colours to its peak and let no enemy ever haul them down."

The three smaller forts in the Bay remained. On Caballo and El Fraile, horrible measures were taken to break the resistance of the Japanese when they refused to surrender. Diesel oil was pumped into their positions and ignited with phosphorus shells and fused T.N.T.; Caballo was cleared on April 13, El Fraile on the 18th. The Japanese evacuated the third island, Canabao, and the Americans encountered no resistance when they landed there on April 16.

Three months after the first American landings in Lingayen Gulf the Japanese had been forced out of central Luzon, the capital had been liberated, and Manila Bay was clear to Allied shipping. But still the battle for Luzon was far from over. Yamashita still had 172,000 Japanese troops under arms. They held the north and south-east of the island; Manila itself was still within range of Japanese guns, and the dams and reservoirs containing the bulk of the capital's water supplies were still in Japanese hands.

Moreover, the Japanese still controlled the most direct sea route through the central Philippines, forcing any Allied shipping heading west for Manila to take an expensive 500-mile detour. Until these problems had been solved and Yamashita's forces had been ground down to total impotence, there could be no question of taking the next step towards Tokyo. The last stage of the battle for Luzon began.

The most urgent problem facing the 6th Army was the big Japanese concentration east of Manila. This was the "Shimbu" Group, under the command of Lieutenant-General Shizuo Yokoyama: 80,000-odd troops, based on the 8th and 105th

Divisions. The bulk of the "Shimbu" Group, 30,000 strong, was dug in along the southern end of the Sierra Madre range along the line Ipo Dam–Wawa Dam–Antipolo, extending south to the great lake of Laguna de Bay. Griswold and XIV Corps launched the first determined narrow-front attack against this strong position on March 8, following two days of intense softening-up by Kenney's bombers. By the 12th, the 1st Cavalry Division had battered its way through the maze of fiercely-defended Japanese cave defences and was relieved on the 13th by the 43rd Division, which kept up the pressure and, in conjunction with 6th Division, punched deep into the centre of the "Shimbu" Group's line. On the 14th, General Hall's XI Corps relieved Griswold on this front and continued the offensive. By the end of March, the 43rd Division had struggled through to the east side of Laguna de Bay and had completely unhinged Yokoyama's left.

Further to the north, however, the 6th Division failed in its drive to capture Wawa and Ipo Dams. It took the whole of April, in the face of implacable Japanese resistance, for the 6th Division to struggle forward into position for a final assault. By this time the successes in the south enabled the 43rd Division to be switched north to add more weight to the next attack.

This was heralded by three days of saturation bombing which dumped 250,000 gallons of napalm on the Japanese positions. The attack proper was launched on the night of May 6 by the 43rd Division. In this battle the American forces were aided to the north by 3,000 Filipino guerrillas, who kept Yokoyama's left flank fully engaged. At last, on May 17, joint American and Filipino attacks seized Ipo Dam intact. Further south, the 6th Division

was relieved by the 38th Division, which ground away at the exhausted Japanese. Finally American persistance told, and the "Shimbu" Group's survivors began to melt away. Wawa Dam fell — also intact — on May 28, by which time the "Shimbu" Group had been destroyed.

By this time, too, the lesser problem of the "Kembu" Group, west of Clark Field, had also been solved. While the bulk of Griswold's corps prepared for the final advance on Manila at the end of January, the 40th Division had been left to mask the "Kembu" force of 25,000 in the heights to which it had retreated after the loss of Clark Field. Here, too, the Japanese made the fullest use of their advantage in terrain and it took over two months of concentrated pressure by three American divisions — first the 40th, then the 43rd and finally the 38th – before Tsukada accepted the inevitable. On April 6 he ordered his surviving forces to go over to independent guerrilla warfare.

Two more Japanese concentrations south of Manila were also successfully broken up in these gruelling weeks. These were the "Fuji" Force commanded by Colonel Fujishige — an Army/Navy agglomeration of about 13,000 men, originally part of "Shimbu" Group-and 3,000 Army and Navy troops down on the Bicol Peninsula, the south-eastern "tail" of Luzon. Again, it was a story of repeated battles throughout February and March, with Filipino guerrillas working in coordination with the regular American forces. By the end of April "Fuji" Force had gone the same way as the "Kembu" Group, while an amphibious landing at Legaspi on the Bicol Peninsula by the 158th Regimental Combat Team had battered west and joined up with 1st Cavalry Division. Southern

Luzon was free.

But the greatest obstacle of all remained: Yamashita and the 110,000 troops of the "Shobu" Group in the north. While the battles in the centre and south of Luzon continued, it was impossible for Krueger to send more than three divisions against Yamashita : the 33rd, 32nd, and 25th. Aided by the 37th Division, the 33rd pushed forward to take Baguio, Yamashita's former H.Q., on April 26; but it took the whole of May and June for Swift's I Corps to break across the Balete Pass, take Bambang, and push on into the Cagayan valley. Airborne forces were dropped at the northern end of the Cagayan valley towards the end of June; they drove south and joined up with 37th Division at Tuguegarao on June 26.

By the end of June Yamashita had 65,000 men still under arms. They had been forced back into the mountains to the south of Bontoc and although it was now quite impossible for them to make any effective challenge to the American hold on Luzon, they nevertheless held out until the end of the war and kept four divisions tied down in consequence. Of all the Japanese forces told to hold the Philippines for the Emperor, Yamashita's men were the ones who came closest to fulfilling their mission.

Thus by the end of June 1945 the battle of Luzon was over. It had been a unique struggle, the most "European" battle of the entire Pacific war. Fought out on an island the size of Britain, it had seen tank battles, amphibious landings, paratroop drops and guerrilla warfare, with a bloody street battle as well. Japanese losses were immense, totalling around 190,000. American losses were 8,000 killed and 30,000 wounded. Further hard fighting lay ahead before the Pacific war would be brought to its close. But there would never be another conflict like the fight for Luzon.

MacArthur had never been ordered to liberate the entire Philippine archipelago. In fact, the British had been told by General Marshall that once the vital objectives had been secured in the Philippines, the liberation of the smaller islands would be left to the Filipinos themselves, with no major American forces taking part. But MacArthur had other ideas; and as long as it was clear that there were no other major objectives for the considerable American land, sea, and air forces in the Philippine area, he was allowed to have his way.

The clearing of the central and southern Philippines was entrusted to the U.S. 8th Army, under Lieutenant-General Robert L. Eichelberger, whose first task was to clear the short-cut sea route through the Visayan Passages. This began with a landing on the north-west coast of Samar on February 19 to clear the San Bernardino Strait and it continued through the month of March, with the occupation of small islands such as Burias, Siniara, Romblon, and Tablas. The last in the sequence was Masbate, and on April 5 Eichelberger reported to MacArthur that the Visayan Passages had been cleared.

In the meantime, the liberation of the key islands in the central and southern Philippines had already begun.

Eichelberger's opponent in the area was the commander of the Japanese 35th Army: Lieutenant-General Sosaku Suzuki. His forces numbered 100,000, dotted over scores of islands, unable to concentrate or assist each other, but prepared to put up as tenacious a fight as their colleagues on Luzon. And fight they did.

By the middle of April Eichelberger's forces had made a grand total of 38 amphibious landings in the central and southern Philippines. None was on the same scale as Leyte or Luzon — but each met with resistance that was no less determined.

Palawan was the first major target: 270 miles long, the westernmost outrider of the Philippine archipelago. The American 186th Regimental Combat Team from the 41st Division landed on Palawan on February 28, but it took it over a week to break the resistance of the 1,750 Army and Navy troops on the island. On March 20 an airstrip at Puerto Princesa began to function.

Ten days before this, however, the rest of the 41st Division had descended on the westernmost tip of Mindanao, second largest and most southerly of the Philippine group. The long, thin Zamboanga Peninsula was their objective, but again it took over two weeks of fighting before their foothold was secure. In the meantime, 41st Division units had been detached to clean out the Sulu Archipelago, the string of diminutive islands stretched between Mindanao and Borneo. This started easily — Basilan, nearest island in the Sulu group to Zamboanga, was unoccupied — but Jolo, in the centre of the chain, was another matter. It was held by 4,000 Japanese troops who fought hard for three weeks after the landing went in on April 9. Even after the main resistance was broken mopping-up continued in the interior of Jolo until July.

Next came the turn of the southern Visayas, four medium-sized islands on roughly the same latitude: from east to west, Bohol, Cebu, Negros, and Panay. Eichelberger divided this group into two, aided by the mountain spine of Negros which partitions the island into Negros Occidental and Negros Oriental. Panay and western Negros were given to the 40th Division; eastern Negros, Cebu, and Bohol to the American Division, originally raised in New Caledonia from non-divisional units in the Pacific theatre, and veterans of Guadalcanal, Bougainville, and Leyte.

The 40th Division landed on Panay on March 18 and wasted no time in completing its assignment. It was considerably helped by strong guerrilla forces; they took Panay's largest port, Iloilo, on the 20th, crossed straight to the island of Guimaras, and landed on the western coast of Negros on March 29. Surprise had been their biggest ally to date, but awaiting them was the biggest Japanese force in the Visayas: 13,500 Army and airforce troops commanded by Lieutenant-General Takeshi Kono. A prolonged battle lasted through April and May before Kono made the inevitable decision to take to the mountains. Over 6,000 of his men were still alive when the war ended.

By far the biggest fight in the Visayas fell to the Americal Division, which landed near Cebu City on March 26. There it found formidable defences, including mined beaches — an obstacle which 8th Army forces had not had to tackle before. A fortnight's hard fighting was needed to prise the Japanese out of their defences and start the mopping-up — but, once again, the Japanese were still holding out in June. In the meantime, Americal troops had subdued Bohol in a mere two weeks after their landing on April 11, and had crossed to eastern Negros, where they joined 40th Division in hunting down the last 1,300 Japanese troops still on the run.

After the- clearing of the Visayas and the Sulu Archipelago, only Mindanao remained: Mindanao, second largest island in the Philippines, and the island which MacArthur had originally planned to liberate first. It was a formidable obstacle. Suzuki had placed over half the 35th Army on Mindanao, intending to make the island the last bastion of Japanese resistance in the Philippines. He did not live to fight this last-ditch battle himself, as he was killed by American aircraft in April. His successor was Lieutenant-General Gyosaku Morozumi, who took over the 43,000 men of the garrison.

Despite the imposing size of their forces on Mindanao, the Japanese only controlled about five per cent of the island. The remainder was under the virtual control of the best equipped,

US troops swarm ashore in Manila.

organised, and led guerrilla forces in the Philippines, under the command of Colonel Wendell W. Fertig. The fact remained, however, that the Japanese held all the populated areas of Mindanao-hence MacArthur's determination to oust them.

The battle for Mindanao began on April 17, 1945, when General Sibert's X Corps landed at Illana Bay. Driving rapidly inland, Sibert's forces covered 115 miles in 15 days and pounced on Davao, depriving the Japanese of their last major town in the Philippines. Davao fell on May 3, but over a month of hard fighting in the hills of the interior lay ahead. Subsequent landings on the north coast of Mindanao, at Macalajar Bay and Butuan Bay, sent further American columns inland to split up the Japanese mass, which was not disrupted and forced into the jungle until the last week of June.

There remained some 2,000 Japanese in the extreme south of the island, who had been cut off there ever since Sibert's pounce on Davao in April-May. These fugitives were the objective of the last seaborne landing of the long struggle for the Philippines which had begun in Leyte Gulf in October 1944. On July 12 a battalion of the 24th Division went ashore to work with the local Filipino guerrillas in rounding up the Japanese. And they landed in Sarangani Bay, the southernmost inlet on Mindanao's coast. Once MacArthur had planned to launch the reconquest of the Philippines at this point. Instead it was the scene of the very last action in the campaign.

Iwo Jima

As a piece of real estate, Iwo Jima has little to offer anyone: it is an island 4 2/3 miles long and 2½ miles wide at its southern end, dominated by the 550-foot high Mount Suribachi, an extinct volcano. There are some sulphur deposits, a plain of black volcanic sand, and in the north a plateau of ridges and gorges between 340 and 368 feet high. In 1944 there were five villages on the island, in the centre and to the north of the plateau.

The importance of the island to both the Japanese and the Americans lay in the two airfields that had been built, and the third under construction, by the Japanese. From these bases Japanese aircraft could intercept the B-29's bombing Japan, and operate against the bomber bases in the Marianas. The island, if captured, would provide the U.S. with a fighter base and emergency landing strips for crippled bombers.

The island's commander, Lieutenant-General Tadamichi Kuribayashi, was fully aware of the island's importance, and set out a series of "Courageous Battle Vows" for the defenders. One of these was "Above all, we shall dedicate ourselves and our entire strength to the defence of the islands."

Kuribayashi's men worked hard, and by the summer of 1944 had driven tunnels through the plateau, laid minefields, and built gun and machine gun emplacements. U.S. reconnaissance aircraft and submarines located 642 blockhouses before the landings.

Never loath to expend vast amounts of material in an effort to spare the lives of their men, the Americans began early with the bombardment of Iwo Jima. On June 15, 1944, carrier planes struck at the island. The attacks continued during the rest of the year, reaching a climax with continuous strikes for 74 days by Saipan-based bombers. The final three-day naval bombardment was carried out by six battleships and their support elements.

The leading wave of L.V.T.s hit the beach at 0902 hours on February 19, 1945 to the north-east of Mt. Suribachi and began immediately to claw its way up the black sand.

The assault troops were men of the 4th Marine (Major-General Clifton B. Cates) and 5th Marine (Major-General Keller E. Rockey) Divisions, both part of Major-General Harry Schmidt's V 'Phib. Corps. The 3rd Marine Division (Major-General Graves B. Erskine) was in corps reserve. In overall command was Lieutenant-General Holland M. Smith.

The troops had practised landings on a similar stretch of beach, and had "stormed" a hill resembling Mount Suribachi. Reconnaissance had also given them some idea of the strength of the defences and the initial bombardment had blown away some of the camouflage, and exposed further emplacements. But what they did not know was that their adversaries had built what was probably the most complex defence system in the Pacific. Although only eight square miles in area, Iwo had 800 pillboxes and three miles of tunnels (Kuribayashi had planned 18). Guns were carefully sited to cover the beaches and a series of inland defence lines. The formation entrusted with the defence, the 109th Division, had 13,586 men by February l, and there were also some 7,347 Navy troops on the island. There were 361 guns of over 75-mm calibre (with 100,000 rounds of ammunition), 300 A.A. guns (150,000 rounds), 20,000 light guns and machine guns (22 million rounds), 130 howitzers (11,700 rounds), 12 heavy mortars (800 rounds), 70 rocket launchers (3,500 rounds), 40 47-mm antitank guns (600 rounds), 20 37-mm antitank guns (500 rounds), and 22 tanks.

Kuribayashi had elected to fight a static battle inshore from the beaches, but the Navy had insisted that possible landing beaches should be covered by bunkers. The Japanese tanks were no match for the American Shermans, and so were positioned hull down in the gullies that scored the island. The gun sites were dug so that the weapon slits were just visible at ground level, and the positions were linked with tunnels. An awesome struggle awaited the Americans.

The Japanese hit back

Massive air and naval bombardment before the landings on Iwo Jima drove the Japanese into their bunkers, and when the Marines landed, optimists suggested that it might be an easy operation. Indeed, it is hard to imagine that any of the defenders could have survived the bombardment, whose finale had included 1,950 rounds of 16-inch shell, 1,500 of 14-inch, 400 of 12-inch, 1,700 of 8-inch, 2,000 of 6-inch, and 31,000 of 5-inch. It was the heaviest pre-landing bombardment of the war. In addition to shellfire, the Navy had also used aircraft to drop bombs and napalm, and fire a multitude of rockets. But although some of their weapons were destroyed, "the Japanese garrison cozily sat it out in their deep underground shelters".

The first wave of Marines had crossed just 200 yards of the beach when they were caught in a savage cross-fire from hidden machine guns. Simultaneously, mortars firing from pits only a few

Us Sixth Fleet during Iwo Jima landings.

feet wide began to drop bombs on the men and vessels along the shore. The U.S. Marine Corps had embarked on the most costly operation of its history.

Despite the fire from these positions that needed explosives, flame-throwers or tanks to overcome, elements of the 5th Marine Division managed to drive across the island on the morning of D-day. When the advance halted for the night at 1800 the Americans were far short of their objectives, but had managed to isolate Mount Suribachi.

Such was the strength of the Japanese positions, however, that it was not until D + 3 that the extinct volcano was firmly surrounded. The following morning, the 28th Marines (with the

2nd and 3rd Battalions forward and the 1st in reserve) gained 200 yards of the mountain's lower slopes. The next day an air strike by 40 planes preceded an attack that reached the foot of the mountain. On the 23rd a patrol of the 2nd Battalion's Company F reported that the Japanese had gone to ground. A larger patrol reached the rim of the crater and was involved in a brisk fire fight.

This patrol, under Lieutenant Harold G. Shrier, hoisted a small (54 × 28 inch) Stars and Stripes flag. Shortly afterwards a larger flag was obtained from an L.S.T., and Schrier decided that this should be raised instead of the first flag. This was photographed by Joe Rosenthal, an Associated Press photographer. The picture of the six men struggling to drive the pole into the volcanic soil has become a classic of the last war.

On March 1, the 28th Marines were moved to the northern sector, to join battalions of the 23rd, 24th, and 25th Marines (4th Division) and the 26th and 27th Marines (5th Division), which had been entrusted with the task of clearing Airfield No. 1 and driving northwards.

It was a battle in which daily gains were measured in hundreds of yards. On February 21 the 21st Marines (3rd Division) were ordered ashore to help.

On the morning of the 24th, after a 76-minute naval bombardment, an air strike, and fire from Marine artillery, the tanks of the 4th and 5th Divisions moved off. One thrust was directed along the western side, and the other along the eastern side, of the airfield. Mines and anti-tank guns stopped the first, but the second pushed on and began to take Japanese emplacements under close range fire. The 5th Division had gained some 500 yards by the end of the day.

On the same day, the 3rd Marine Division landed. and was allotted the task of driving along the centre of Iwo's northern plateau. Once this was taken, the Marines would be able to push down the spurs leading to the sea. The plateau was an extraordinary feature, eroded into fantastic shapes by wind, rain, and volcanic activity.

The division launched its attack at 0930 on the 25th. It was a slow and costly operation, as the attack met the main Japanese line of defences. Three days of attacks, in which the Marines brought up flame-throwing tanks to incinerate the Japanese in their shell-proof bunkers, finally broke through the line. On the 28th the Marines secured the ruins of Motoyama village and the hills overlooking Airfield No. 3. The Americans now held all three airfields, the objectives of the landings, but the fighting was by no means over.

On the last day of the month, the Marines attacked the two small features of Hills 382 and 362A. Their size was misleading, for each contained a warren of tunnels and bunkers. The crest of Hill 382 had been hollowed out and turned into a huge bunker housing anti-tank guns and other artillery. Tanks were sited in the gullies. To the south of the hill there was a massive rock which became known as Turkey Knob, with a natural bowl christened the Amphitheater. The fighting for both features became so intense that they became known as the Meatgrinder. A series of savage local battles was fought on March 1. And although Hill 382 fell that day, it was not until the 10th that the Japanese defending Turkey Knob and the Amphitheater were destroyed.

Iwo Jima

The attack on the Hill 362A complex on March 2 was a marked departure from normal Marine practice-they attacked at night. Although movement through the rugged terrain was slow and tiring, the tactics surprised the enemy. After a fierce fight on the 8th, the Marines were in possession of the whole area.

Despite the loss of these key points, the Japanese continued to. fight with their customary aggressiveness. On the 8th they launched an attack on the junction between the 23rd and 24th Marines. Caught in the open without artillery support, the attack failed with 650 dead. With this defeat the Japanese defence began to crumble, and the battle moved into the mopping up stage. Individual strongpoints were in no mood to surrender, however, and as they had ample stocks of food, water, and ammunition, they could hold out for some time. Indeed, on March 15, many of the last defenders attempted to infiltrate the American lines.

The last pocket to be destroyed was that at Kitano Point, which was declared officially secure on March 25. But that night over 200 Japanese emerged from the flame-blackened and shell-scarred rocks. Led in person by Kuribayashi, some say, they tore into the bivouac area occupied by the sleeping men of the 5th Pioneer Battalion. A defensive line was set up. by the Army's VII Fighter Command and the Marines' 8th Field Depot and by dawn at least 223 Japanese, including their leader, lay dead.

The conquest of Iwo Jima had cost the Marines 5,931 dead and 17,372 wounded. But by the end of the war the island's airfields had saved the lives of 24,761 American pilots and aircrew. Of the 21,000 Japanese defending the island, only 216 were taken prisoner. If this was the cost of taking an island of only eight square miles and which had been Japanese only since 1891, what would be the cost of the conquest of Japan?

US troops raising US flag on Mount Suribachi, Iwo Jima

Throughout World War II, the vital problem of transporting supplies into China loomed large. In 1937–39, during the undeclared Sino-Japanese war, the occupation of the coasts of China by the Japanese stimulated intensive efforts to build supply routes from the interior of China to the outside world. Perhaps the most notable of these was the construction by the British and Chinese of the 681-mile road from the Lashio railhead to Muse on the China-Burma border, and on to Kunming. This highway, called the Burma Road, was made passable to motor transport in 1938 by the labours of thousands of Chinese coolies, and for three years, the Burma Road shuddered with the passage of several thousand trucks carrying war supplies to China. Contemporary Burmese political leaders, however, regarded operations on this road with very little enthusiasm, the desire to keep the doors of Burma shut against foreign intruders being an old theme in Burmese history.

China was dependent on supplies from abroad to enable her to continue in the war against Japan. As well as the Burma Road route, a trickle of supplies also reached China along the narrow-gauge railway from Haiphong, in French Indo-China, to Kunming. With the defeat of France in Europe, though, Japan demanded and received from the Vichy Government the right to land forces in French Indo-China. The Haiphong-Kunming railway was closed in June 1940. The Japanese followed this by demanding the closure of the Burma Road, and on July 18, 1940, Britain, hard pressed by Germany, reluctantly complied. China was now virtually isolated, but Generalissimo Chiang Kai-shek and the Chinese people remained steadfast.

The Burma Road, fortunately, did not remain closed for long. Britain defeated Germany in the Battle of Britain, and Churchill, with the backing of the United States, which wished to ship Lend-Lease supplies to China, ordered the reopening of the Road on October 18, 1940. This was now the only supply route to China, and large quantities of American Lend-Lease military supplies began to arrive in Rangoon. From here, they travelled by steamer up the Irrawaddy, and by road and rail north through Mandalay to Lashio where they joined the Burma Road.

Air support from the "Flying Tigers"

Air-power is important in any theatre of war, but in Burma it was a dominating factor from the start. In planning at this time, great reliance was placed on the ability of air forces to halt, or at least to delay greatly, the advance of enemy columns. Over the next three years, however, this was shown to be a fallacy. Air attack alone could not stop the movement of either side. Even if it could, the Anglo-American air forces in Burma were not then of a size to attempt it. The air force in Burma consisted of only one R.A.F. squadron, equipped with Buffaloes, and a flight of the Indian Air Force having only a few obsolete machines. The Chinese Air Force also had a handful of antiquated planes. To redeem this situation, the American Volunteer Group (A.V.G.) was formed by Colonel Claire Chennault, Chiang Kai-shek's aeronautics adviser, its major task being to protect the Burma Road, which was extremely vulnerable to air attack. The A.V.G. base was in Kunming, China, but Chiang, realising the importance of Rangoon for the Burma Road, sent the 3rd Squadron of the A.V.G. to R.A.F. Mingaladon,

Chinese workders stand on edge of field to watch take-off of Flying Tiger, Burma, 1944.

range, but by February 12, 1942, the Flying Tigers had shot down almost 100 enemy planes for the loss of only 15 of their own, spurred on, no doubt, by a reward of 500 dollars for every Japanese plane downed.

On December 23, 1941, the Japanese launched their first raid on Rangoon. On January 20, 1942, after almost a month of bombing raids against Rangoon and other military installations in Burma, Japanese land forces crossed the Thai border into southern Burma. Their purpose was to cut the link between Rangoon and Kunming and then to capture Burma. Rangoon was captured on March 6, 1942, and Lashio, the southern terminus of the Burma Road, fell on April 29, along with 44,000 tons of Lend-Lease supplies destined for China.

Japanese forces cut the Road

With the closing of the Burma Road, the only land routes to China were the old highway across the Sinkiang province from Russia, and the caravan trails across the Himalayas and through Tibet from India. Neither of these routes was ideal for transporting large quantities of goods to China. The route through Sinkiang was over thousands of miles of overloaded Russian railways, and although the caravan route through Tibet was a much shorter journey, only pack animals could traverse the mountain trails, which meant that heavy equipment could not be carried.

near Rangoon. If the Japanese succeeded in occupying Burma and closing the Road, China's ability to resist Japan would be greatly diminished. The defence of Burma was thus imperative. Without the flow of supplies over the Burma Road, the likelihood that the A.V.G. could continue to function effectively in China was nil.

The A.V.G. was equipped with 100 P-40 Tomahawk aircraft, supplied by America through Lend-Lease, and the airmen were hand-picked volunteers from the American air force. The pilots decorated their planes, which were consequently known as the "Flying Tigers".

The Allied air forces were contending against great odds, however. The Japanese aircraft were superior in number and

Chinese nationalist troops load an 82mm mortar for assault on Japanese.

"The Hump"

The fall of Lashio was therefore a crushing blow to the Chinese, but they survived it through the establishment of the air lift over the "Hump" from India to China.

Pioneers over the Himalayan Hump to China from India were Colonels Old and Tate. After Colonel Old had made the first surveying flight, Colonel Tate proved it was usable by transporting 13,000 Chinese troops to General Stilwell in India during the 1942 monsoon season.

Operating between 16,000 and 22,000 feet with oxygen, the pilots flew through almost all weather, although sometimes monsoon rains and wind delayed the flights for days at a time. When the accident rate became high, Chinese pickets were paid so much for every pilot saved. Although the tonnage carried over the "Hump" was low in the beginning, the Americans stepped up the monthly average to 20,000 tons during 1943.

Even when the planes made their regular journeys, however, there were difficulties in moving the goods from Kunming to the forward bases of the China Air Task Force, which were situated in regions surrounded by Japanese, and defended only by poorly equipped Chinese armies. The China Air Task Force had superseded the A.V.G. in July 1942, and most of the "Hump" supplies were allotted to it as Chiang Kai-shek and Chennault believed that decisive results could be achieved through airpower alone.

For raids against Japanese installations in Burma, China, and Indo-China, the China Air Task Force needed a large amount of aviation gasoline. With the closing of the Burma Road, all fuel had to be flown in over the "Hump"; then it had to be carried or rolled by Chinese coolies over hundreds of miles of dirt road to reach the air bases. To carry one day's supply of fuel from Kunming to Kuei-lin took 40 days if carried by cart, and 75 days if rolled by coolies.

On March 10, 1943, the China Air Task Force was enlarged and redesignated the 14th Air Force, still under the command of Chennault. Fuel was in very short supply at this time, not so much because of an insufficient number of planes to ferry goods to China, but due to bottlenecks along the route from Calcutta and Karachi to the airfields in Assam. Indian rail facilities were disorganised and inadequate to convey large quantities of goods quickly. There was also a delay on the part of the British to complete the necessary airfields in Assam on time.

The "Hump" air lift enabled the Chinese to receive supplies to continue in the war. What had happened to the land forces in the meanwhile?

The land force commanders

In the last days of April 1942, the commanders of the Allied forces in Burma and China (Slim, Stilwell, and Alexander) realised that they could no longer hold any line against the Japanese in Burma. The troops therefore withdrew to India, to do so undertaking a 20-day journey of hard foot-slogging through 140 miles of jungle and mountain.

On arriving in Delhi, Stilwell stated that he regarded Burma as a vitally important area for re-entry into China, and that it must be recaptured. Stilwell's determination and implacable will were to be one of the constants during the Allied planning for the return to Burma.

While the British and Chinese forces were struggling through the mountains into Assam, there were still six Chinese divisions in operation in eastern Burma, being vigorously pursued by the enemy. In the middle of May, it appeared that the Japanese were about to launch a major attack up the Burma Road, advance into Yunnan, and capture the terminus of the Road. They did not in fact do this, and later they denied they had any plans to do so, but Chiang and Chennault were convinced that a major attack was imminent. Before the end of April, Japanese units were pushing north from Lashio up the Burma Road with tanks and motorised infantry. Having swept aside Chinese opposition, they reached the gorge of the Salween river. Their advance was halted here, however, when the Chinese destroyed the bridge.

By the end of May the Japanese held Burma and were in a dominating strategic position. Though temporarily checked by monsoon rains, they were poised to attack either India or China, and could certainly bomb Calcutta, where most of the American and British supplies were concentrated.

Various plans were put forward at this time for the recapture of Burma. The American priority was supplies for China, by road or air, and they therefore wanted the offensive to take place in

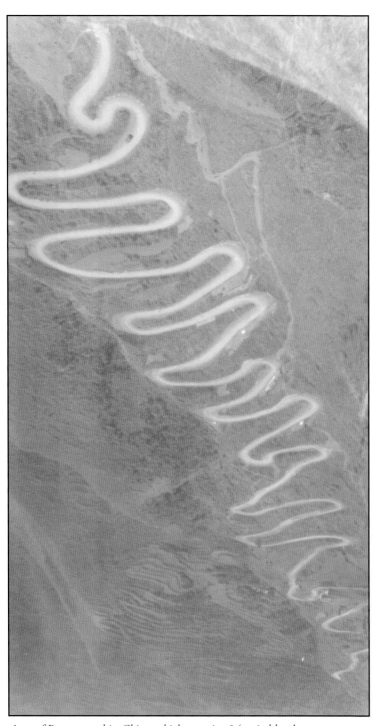

Area of Burma road in China which contains 24 switchbanks.

northern Burma. The Americans also favoured the construction of a new overland route to China, and planned a route for this. The British, too, had a projected road plan, but the American one was chosen, and the building of the road was assigned to the Americans. They possessed the necessary manpower, materials, and engineering experience on a large scale. Stilwell was made responsible for the road. The plans were drawn up by Brigadier-General Raymond Wheeler. American engineers, under the command of Colonel Arrowsmith and later General Pick, commenced work on the road on Christmas Day 1942, cutting the first trace at Milestone Zero, just outside Ledo. They aimed at reaching Shinbwiyang, 103 miles away at the head of the Hukawng valley, within a year.

The Ledo Road project was an ambitious scheme. It aimed at cutting a three-lane highway in gravel from Ledo, the railway terminus in north Assam, through the Patkai hills in north Burma, down the Hukawng valley to Myitkyina, across the Irrawaddy to Bhamo, where it would join up with the old British road from Bhamo to Namkham. It would then go on to the little village of Mong Yaw where it would meet the old Burma Road. The overall distance to the Chinese border was 478 miles. The eventual destination of the convoys, starting from Ledo, was Chungking, the Nationalist Chinese capital and Chiang Kai-shek's headquarters, nearly 2,000 miles away.

Building the road involved the most complicated engineering and extreme hazards. The uncharted track led through formidable country with cliffs, enormous peaks, hushed forests, and winding rivers. As well as geographical hazards, there were also extremes of temperature, and disease (including malaria, black-water fever, dysentery, and scrub typhus) was rife. Men fought disease by oiling, disinfecting, and spraying the countryside, but even so the sickness rate was high. Fits of depression were also common to the road builders. Yet progress was made in conditions that at any time other than war would have been intolerable. Life was not eased by the frequent infiltration of Japanese behind the Allied lines: balanced in high trees, they sniped at those working on the road, and seriously hampered progress.

American matériel paves the way

As the American engineering battalions — composed mostly of negroes with a cadre of white operatives — pushed forward, so the stream of men and materiel behind them increased. From America by ship to Karachi and Bombay, then across India by train, came more bulldozers, graders, sifters, caterpillars, medical units, supply units, and transport. From India and the hills, 50,000 coolies came to work on the road.

The monsoon season presented more problems. Rain fell at the rate of up to 15 inches per day, and this led to floods and landslides. Mules and vehicles got bogged down, and bulldozers were lost over collapsing steep banks. The men, wet all the time, slept in waterlogged tents or jungle-hammocks. The soggy jungle became infested with long, purple leeches.

During the monsoon months, though, there was little likelihood of interference from the Japanese north of the Hukawng valley, and the Chinese 38th Division left its Ledo base and was deployed in front of the engineering group as forward protection.

Top priority status allocated

At the "Trident" Conference in May, 1943, the Combined Chiefs-of-Staff urged the importance of operations in northern Burma, and directed that an offensive designed to facilitate the building of the road should begin before the end of the year.

The Ledo Road followed the course of the fighting in Burma through the Hukawng and Mogaung valleys, and on to Myitkyina, which had fallen to Stilwell's Chinese and American troops in the middle of 1944. The road then had to be carried on to Bhamo, from where the Japanese had withdrawn, and then on to Namkham.

The Stilwell Road opens to traffic

On January 31, 1945, a ceremony was held on the Burma-China border at Wan-t'ing chen. With great fanfare and rejoicing, a convoy, largely composed of American journalists out on a spree, and the Chinese 6th Route Army, left for Kunming. The Ledo Road was now officially open.

Chiang Kai-shek proposed that the combined Burma and Ledo roads be renamed the Stilwell Road in honour of the man who had worked so hard to break the land blockade of China.

The value of the Ledo Road was questioned by some who doubted if it would ever repay the expenditure in men and resources devoted to it. Sadly, in November 1946, the Ledo Road was declared "surplus property" by the United States Army after the altogether vital part it had played in keeping China in the war.

Allies unload supplies at Rangoon beachhead, Burma, 1945.

There has been a tendency among some historians of the Burma campaign to neglect the Allied fighting forces which operated on either side of their advance and give the impression that it was the 14th Army alone who confronted the Japanese armies when they advanced down from Imphal to Mandalay and Rangoon. This, of course, was not the case and it was the Northern Combat Area Command under Stilwell with his three and then five Chinese divisions, coupled with first the Chindit operations and then the operations of the British 36th Division which first penetrated the plains of north Burma and turned the flank of the Japanese 15th Army facing the 14th Army. The ill-equipped 12 Chinese divisions on the River Salween have been denigrated for their lack of initiative and attacking spirit. But it must be remembered that these particular Chinese divisions each amounted to only a weak British brigade in strength, and from their point of view they were hundreds of miles away in a remote corner of China, facing one of the swiftest and most incalculable rivers in the world, the Salween, while the best armies and technical weapons available were being used to combat the 25 Japanese divisions occupying eastern and central China. Whilst the operations described here were going on, the Japanese, incensed by American air attacks from China on shipping in the South China Sea and as far north as Japan itself, attacked and overran the Chinese provinces of Kwangsi and Hunan, an area about the size of France. It must also be remembered that the objectives given to Mountbatten and Stilwell for 1944, to which Stilwell stuck, was the capture of Mogaung and Myitkyina and an area south sufficient to protect those two towns, so that a road and petrol pipeline could be opened to China and help keep her in the war. Stilwell had responsibilities to China as well as South-East Asia.

General Giffard had judged that the Arakan coastal terrain was an area in which it was uneconomic to operate and had, therefore, decided to stop any further attempt to advance there. But when Mountbatten, who was still without sufficient landing craft to capture Rangoon, was given permission to conquer Burma from the north, he found that he was faced with a big logistic problem. Once the 14th Army, with its 260,000 troops, crossed the Irrawaddy, their communications to a railhead and air bases in Assam lengthened to such an extent that they became uneconomic. It was, therefore, necessary to capture and develop airfields along the coast of Burma which could be supplied easily by sea, so that Slim's 14th Army could in turn be supplied from there by air. Thus plans were made to expand the port and airfields at Chittagong and to capture Akyab and Ramree Islands.

The 14th Army had started to cross the Chindwin early in December 1944 and Major-General T. W. Rees's 19th Indian Division, which had never been in action before, quickly crossed the formidable Zibyu Taungdan Range and made contact at Wuntho on the railway with Festing's British 36th Division.

Messervy's race for Meiktila

Slim's plan was to destroy the Japanese 15th Army between the hammer of Stopford's XXXIII Corps advancing on Mandalay and the armoured anvil of Messervy's IV Corps which was to capture Meiktila.

This plan depended on the speed and secrecy of Messervy's 150-mile advance west of the Irrawaddy, whilst Stopford held the attention of XV Corps near Mandalay. Rees's 19th Division, to the north of Mandalay, was still the main attraction for the Japanese. Stopford's 20th Division started to cross the Irrawaddy at Myinmu on February 12 at a point about 30 miles downstream from Mandalay. This immediately attracted the Japanese, who counter-attacked the bridgehead repeatedly for the next two weeks.

Stopford's British 2nd Division had to wait for the boats and pontoon rafts used by the 20th Division before they could start to cross on February 21 at Ngazun at a point 15 miles from Mandalay. Unfortunately, many of the boats and pontoons had been inadvertently damaged by the 20th Division and the 2nd Division had a difficult crossing. However, these assault crossings achieved the desired strategic effect of attracting the full attention of the tiny Japanese 15th Army, so that when Messervy's 7th Division crossed 90 miles further south on February 13, there was little or no opposition. By the end of February Slim's 14th Army had crossed the 1,000-yard wide swift-flowing Irrawaddy in four places with his northern bridgeheads attracting a violent reaction from the Japanese.

Messervy built up his bridgehead at Nyangu before he made his dash to Meiktila. By February 20 Messervy had got his 17th Division and 255th Tank Brigade across the Irrawaddy into his bridgehead at Nyangu, and was ready to start. Meiktila was 80 miles away across sandy scrub country, broken up by dry river beds. On February 21 Messervy's tanks began to roll. At the same time Major-General G. C. Evans's 7th Division, which had carried out the crossing, was ordered to capture the oil town of Chauk and lead on to Myingyan to the north east. Major-General D. T. Cowan's 17th Division, with its tank brigade, reached the outskirts of Meiktila by the end of February and on March 1, Cowan attacked.

Meiktila fell the following day and its airfield on the eastern edge of the town, which was vital for re-supply and the reinforcement of the defence, was captured on March 3. Cowan did not settle down but immediately sent out fighting patrols of tanks and infantry to seek out and find the enemy.

At this vital juncture Slim flew in with Messervy to visit

Cowan and was present to observe a quite severe Japanese counter-attack, in which the British tanks caused many casualties and dispersed the attackers. Two men in the army commander's party were wounded by Japanese artillery fire but Slim, Messervy, and Cowan stood unmoved on the hilltop like Old Testament prophets whilst their men below gained victory.

After a new brigade was flown in Cowan withstood a series of local Japanese counter-attacks. Meanwhile to the north, Stopford, having seen his bridgeheads were secure, made plans for a deliberate advance to capture Mandalay. His plan was that the 19th Division would attack from the north. The 2nd Division would advance through the old capital of Ava along the Irrawaddy from the west and the 20th Division would sweep round the south to attack Mandalay from the south and the south-east. The 19th Division soon penetrated the town but was held up by defences on Mandalay Hill and the battlements of Fort Dufferin. The 2nd Division was delayed amongst the pagodas of Ava, but the 20th Division made good progress around the south where the opposition was negligible.

As soon as Slim realised that Mandalay was not held in strength, he ordered the 20th Division to send a column south towards Meiktila, leaving the British 2nd Division to surround it from the south.

What was left of the 15th Army in Mandalay was destroyed by heavy bomber attacks. Mandalay became a bomb trap. Meiktila had fallen on March 1 and Mandalay fell on March 20.

At this time the Japanese Intelligence had become completely confused and they did not seem to know what was hitting them and from where. The battles for Meiktila and Mandalay were the death knell of the already depleted 15th Army. In mid-January the Yunnan Armies at last began to advance across the Salween. Namkham and Wamting were soon captured. By January 18 the American "Mars" Force was overlooking the Mandalay-Lashio road at Hsenwi and was carrying out guerrilla raids along it. On January 21 the Ledo Road to China via Bhamo, Namkham, Muse, and Wamting was opened, followed by the first convoy to China, which arrived at Kunming on February 4.

This date, February 4, 1945, can be said, therefore, to be the date of the completion of the "Quadrant" plan. However, Chiang Kai-shek made this the occasion to start to withdraw his Yunnan armies back into China for the very sensible reason that he wanted now to retake the huge areas of China which the Japanese had recently overrun. This was naturally supported by the Americans, who required these areas for air bases to support their advance towards the invasion of Japan. But some of the more parochial commanders in A.L.F.S.E.A. tended to denigrate the Chinese for marching away from the "battlefields in Burma", perhaps forgetting that the Chinese had been fighting since 1937.

The final stages

Mandalay may have fallen, but Stilwell's forces were still active. By March 1 the Chinese 30th Division had occupied Hsenwi and the British 36th Division was crossing the Shweli at Myitson and Mongmit against the now 3,000-strong 18th Division. The British received 360 casualties during this crossing.

On March 6 the Chinese 38th Division occupied Lashio and

by March 24 the Burma Road from Mandalay to Lashio was in Allied hands. The British 36th Division, having captured the ruby mine town of Mogok on March 19, moved to Mandalay when the Northern Combat Area Command ceased to exist.

The American "Mars" Force, the worthy successors of Merrill's Marauders, was moved to China to be dispersed into training cadres to rebuild the Chinese Army along the same lines as Stilwell's Chinese New Armies.

Thus ended the American army involvement in the war in Burma. It can be said with truth that the few representatives of the American army, Merrill's Marauders and "Mars" Force, gave a very good impression by their fighting capabilities and thrustful initiative to their Allies fighting in Burma.

Parts of the Japanese 33rd Army had been moved from the Lashio Road at the end of the Meiktila battle in a vain attempt to save the town. But even with this last-minute reinforcement, the British forces outnumbered their enemy by about ten to one on the ground and about twenty to one in tanks.

IV Corps casualties from the crossing of the Irrawaddy to the end of March were 835 killed, 3,174 wounded, and 90 missing. The high proportion of wounded was because in the Indian Army, anyone who incurred a wound obtained a pension, and so the smallest wounds were noted, whereas in the British units there was no point in worrying about or recording minor wounds. During these battles IV Corps had 26 tanks destroyed and 44 damaged.

XXXIII Corps, in its capture of Mandalay, lost 1,472 killed and 4,933 wounded, with 120 missing. It had one more division than IV Corps and was in action for six weeks before IV Corps

Allied troops engage in combat, Mandalay, Burma 1945.

had crossed the Irrawaddy, so that the proportion of casualties is comparable.

No. 221 Group (Air Vice-Marshal S. F. Vincent) was in support throughout and flew 4,360 sorties, of which 2,085 were attacks on Japanese positions or their communications, during which 1,560 tons of bombs were dropped.

The 14th Army was now all set for its dash to capture Rangoon and obtain a port before the monsoon. The opposition to its advance was now negligible from the battered Japanese forces.

The build-up of Allied naval forces resulted in the command of the Indian Ocean and the Bay of Bengal being regained by the

A Japanese headquarters burns after an attack by allied Beaufighters, Burma.

Allies by the beginning of 1945. This made possible not only the more rapid reinforcement of India because troopships were able to sail independently without escort, but amphibious operations could now be undertaken along the coast of Burma without fear of heavy losses to submarines, and without the need for powerful naval covering forces.

Lieutenant-General Sir Philip Christison was given two tasks to carry out. When the 14th Army crossed the Irrawaddy in February 1945 their supply lines to Assam had become uneconomic. It was therefore necessary to capture airfields along the coast of Arakan, from which the 14th Army could be re-supplied during its advance to Meiktila and south to Rangoon. Without these airfields and the necessary sea ports to land stores, the 14th Army could not advance south. Fortunately the Japanese, as a result of the pressure of the 81st West African Division east of them, had evacuated Akyab on December 31 so that Christison's XV Corps landed unopposed on January 2. He immediately arranged to re-open the port of Akyab for supplies.

The total strength of the British portion of A.L.F.S.E.A. (that is not including the Americans and Chinese) was, by the beginning of 1945, 971,828 men, including 127,139 British troops, 581,548 Indians, 44,988 East Africans, 59,878 West Africans, and 158,275 civilian labourers. Of these, 260,000 were in the 14th Army, including its line of communications troops. It was calculated, therefore, that in order to supply the 14th Army as well as XV Corps, whose secondary rôle was to try to contain all Japanese forces (including the 54th Division and remnants of the 55th Division) in the area and to try to prevent their being re-deployed in the Irrawaddy valley, it was necessary to open two new ports. The first was at Akyab, and the second at Kyaukpyu on Ramree Island. From these two ports and from Chittagong the divisions of the 14th Army in central Burma, and the formations of XV Corps operating on the Arakan coast could be maintained if the ports could be built up to a capacity sufficient to handle the necessary sea lift tonnage required.

It was calculated that the port of Akyab would have to maintain 46,000 men, as well as the construction stores required for two all-weather airfields and the tonnage necessary to build up a 20,000-ton reserve for the 14th Army. This would require a maximum sea lift of 850 tons a day in February and March 1945, dropping down to 600 tons in May when the unnecessary formations of XV Corps, having achieved their object, were sent back to India.

In the same manner it was calculated that the port of Kyaukpyu must maintain 36,000 men from February to May and handle stores sufficient to construct two all-weather airfields and build up a stockpile of 22,000 tons for the 14th Army. The daily sealift required would be 450 tons in February, rising to 650 tons from March to May.

Lieutenant-General M. Kawabe had ordered the 28th Army (Lieutenant-General S. Sakurai) to send its 2nd Division, with a large part of the army's motor transport, to the 33rd Army, which was facing the 14th Army, and to hold with his remaining two divisions (54th and 55th) the Irrawaddy delta and the Arakan coast up to 35 miles north of Kyaukpyu. Later the 2nd Division was to move to Indo-China.

Sakurai was told to hold the offshore islands of Cheduba and Ramree for as long as possible. The removal of the Japanese 2nd Division (on its way to Indo-China), which had previously been responsible for the delta and the remainder of the Burmese coastline further south, meant that Sakurai had to withdraw his 55th Division to protect that area, leaving the 54th Division to face Christison's XV Corps.

Lieutenant-General S. Miyazaki's 54th Division had received orders in December 1944 to protect the rear of the 15th Army in the Irrawaddy valley from any risks of XV Corps cutting their communications between Meiktila and Rangoon. It will be remembered that Miyazaki had carried out the rear guard action of 33rd Division during its wholesale retreat from Kohima brilliantly.

To carry out his orders, Miyazaki had to hold the An and Taungup passes at all costs. As the 81st and then the 82nd West African Division advanced slowly down the Kaladan, Miyazaki decided that he would use a covering force to delay these two divisions for as long as possible whilst basing his main defence in the north at Kangaw, 40 miles east of Akyab. His other strongpoint would be at Taungup itself. Ten miles west of Kangaw lay the Myebon peninsula.

Before Akyab had fallen Christison had already made plans to land on the Myebon peninsula.

XV Corps consisted of the 25th and 26th Indian Divisions, the 81st and 82nd West African Divisions, and the 3rd Commando Brigade (which was to be increased to four Royal Marine and Army Commandos). Christison now had plenty of landing craft, reinforced with locally constructed craft. Now that the Royal Navy had regained command of the Bay of Bengal and Akyab had fallen, it was possible for XV Corps to advance south. The Myebon peninsula and Ramree Island were held by Japanese outposts covering the main defences on the mainland.

On January 14, the joint force commanders (Rear-Admiral B. C. S. Martin [Flag Officer Force "W"], Lieutenant-General Christison, and Air Vice-Marshal The Earl of Bandon) decided that the 26th Division would assault Ramree on January 21 and the 25th Division (Major-General C. E. N. Lomax) and 3rd Commando Brigade (Brigadier C. R. Hardy) would occupy the

Myebon peninsula and strike east towards Kangaw to cut the Japanese 54th Division's communications to the north.

The 3rd Commando Brigade would spearhead the attack on Myebon with the 74th Brigade passing through.

A reconnaissance of the beaches at Myebon by a special boating party found that a line of coconut stakes had been driven in just below the low-water mark about 300 yards offshore. So before the attack, a Combined Operation Piloted Party (part of the special Small Operations Group) went ashore and attached to these stakes explosives timed to go off at zero hour. The anti-boat stakes were thus blown, tearing a gap 25 yards wide for No. 42 (Royal Marine) Commando to land under cover of a smokescreen laid from the air on the morning of January 12.

The Commandos suffered a few casualties from mines on the beach, but quickly formed a beach-head. The landing was supported by the cruiser Phoebe, the destroyer Napier, the sloops Narbada and Jumna, and four minesweepers. Forty-nine landing craft of all types (including three L.C.I., five L.C.T., 12 L.C.M., and 18 L.C.A.) landed the commandos.

The Royal Marines found that the beach was too muddy for tanks, vehicles, and stores to land so the Royal Engineers reconnoitred and constructed a new route, using explosives to smooth out a nearby rocky outcrop on which tanks and vehicles could land.

Shortly afterwards No. 5 Commando landed and passed through No. 42 Commando to widen the beach-head.

Nos. 1 and 44 (Royal Marine) Commandos also inadvertently landed on the same beach and pushed ahead. By this time the tanks belonging to the 19th Lancers were ashore.

The Royal Marines of No. 42 Commando occupied Myebon village on the 13th and the village of Kantha was also captured. At this stage the 74th Brigade (Brigadier J. E. Hirst) took up the advance and overcame the remaining opposition and the Commando Brigade was withdrawn to prepare for the Kangaw operation. By the 17th the whole of the Myebon peninsula was captured.

The 82nd West African Division had relieved 81st Division, which was still in the Kaladan valley. The 82nd Division was now commanded by Major-General H. C. Stockwell, who had previously commanded one of the aggressive British 36th Division's two brigades. Advancing south, Stockwell occupied the ancient capital of Arakan, Myohaung, on January 25 and applied pressure on the Japanese facing him. Christison was anxious to cripple the 54th Division by cutting its communications at Kangaw.

The joint force commanders rather over-insured in the force that they used to overcome opposition on Ramree and Cheduba Islands. But at this time of the war it was common policy for the Allies to deploy as much matériel strength as possible to save Allied lives if that matériel strength could be easily brought to bear without too much delay.

The naval component of this combined operation included the battleship Queen Elizabeth, the cruiser Phoebe, the destroyers Rapid and Napier, the Royal Naval sloop Flamingo, and the R.I.N. sloop Kistna. No. 224 Group supported the attack with its Thunderbolts and Mitchells. Prior to the attack 85 Liberators of the Strategic Air Command bombarded the beaches and its surrounds.

After the naval and air bombardment, the 71st Brigade (Brigadier R. C. CottrellHill), with a squadron of tanks, a regiment of field artillery, and two companies of the Frontier Force machine gun battalion, landed unopposed at 0942 on January 21 west of the town of Kyaukpyu. The leading motor launch and landing craft both struck mines and were blown up, causing some confusion, but the remainder of the landing proceeded without opposition or further delay.

Next day the 4th Brigade (Brigadier J. F. R. Forman) took over the beachhead and the 71st Brigade moved south.

On January 26 the Royal Marine Commandos landed unopposed on the neighbouring Cheduba Island.

By January 31 Lomax had landed the remainder of his 25th Division on Ramree Island. The opposition from the Japanese outposts increased and the Indian brigades, with tanks, slowly and methodically cleared the island until Ramree town itself was occupied on June 9. On this day, under cover of an attack by the remains of the Japanese 5th Air Division, a Japanese destroyer (accompanied by 20 launches) rushed to the rescue of the Japanese and took off over 500 men. By January 17 resistance on the island ended.

The 22nd East African Brigade, which had come under Christison's command, arrived to garrison Ramree and Cheduba Islands so that the 26th Division would be available to land at Toungup.

The fight at Kangaw turned out to be one of the bloodiest and

Disarmed Japanese leave Rangoon, Burma 1945.

most savage of the Burma campaign. But this fight succeeded in crippling a major part of Miyazaki's 54th Division, which was one of the few divisions in Burma at this time which had not suffered a defeat, was not too depleted, and was still full of fight.

Major-General G. N. Wood's plan for the capture of Kangaw was for the 3rd Commando Brigade (Nos. 1, 5, 42, and 44 Commandos) to seize a bridgehead on the east bank of the Diangbon Chaung two miles south-west of Kangaw. Then his 51st Brigade would pass through the bridgehead and join forces with the 74th Brigade, which was advancing from Kantha across the Min Chaung from the Myebon peninsula. The Japanese would find themselves hemmed in between the two Indian

4-10th Gurkhas arriving in Burma as par to the Allied Force.

brigades and the West African 82nd Division advancing from the north. Hardy, commanding the 3rd Commando Brigade, wished to go by the indirect route, which he had reconnoitred, and advance up the Diangbon Chaung from the south and not via the Myebon peninsula, although this meant a trip of 27 miles by boat. On January 21, 50 vessels (including the R.I.N. sloop Narbada, a minesweeper, a Landing Craft Tank (carrying a bulldozer and R.E. equipment), four L.C.Ls, 22 L.C.A.s, and some "Z" craft carrying artillery, anchored off the southern entrance of the Diangbon Chaung. The "Z" craft were large but manoeuvrable lighters whose decks had been strengthened with steel so that a troop of 25-pounders could fire from them.

The Diangbon Chaung, as Hardy predicted, had not been mined and the Japanese did not see the approach of the attack. The Royal Navy and R.I.N. bombarded the beaches, supported by the medium bombers of No. 224 Group, which also laid a smokescreen. Surprise was complete and No. 1 Commando pushed on to Hill 170 which was to be the scene of heavy fighting. By nightfall No. 5 Commando had landed, with the next day Nos. 44 (R.M.) and 42 (R.M.) Commandos.

The Japanese on the spot counterattacked fiercely and efforts to infiltrate the village of Kangaw were rebuffed. The Japanese heavily bombarded the beaches with field artillery on the 24th and 25th, but on the 26th the 51st Brigade (Brigadier R. A. Hutton) landed with a troop of medium tanks followed by the 53rd Brigade (Brigadier B. C. H. Gerty).

As soon as he heard of the landing, General Miyazaki ordered Major-General T. Koba, commanding the "Matsu" Detachment, to repel the invaders and keep open the road. Koba, as a colonel, had commanded the two battalion column which had so successfully driven the 81st West African Division out of the Kaladan in March 1944. The "Matsu" Detachment consisted of the 54th Infantry Group, comprising three infantry battalions and an artillery battalion. Koba arrived on January 31 and immediately launched a heavy attack on Hill 170, which was held by Nos. 1 and 42 Royal Marine Commandos, commanded by Colonel Peter Young, Hardy's second in command.

The Commandos, supported by three tanks, repulsed Koga's most determined assaults. Attack and counter-attack waged around Hill 170 for 36 hours. The "Matsu" Detachment finally launched a pole-charge tank hunting party of engineers. They destroyed two tanks and damaged the third with a loss of 70 of their own men killed. By this time the 74th Brigade was moving in from the north-west: but not before the Commandos had killed over 300 Japanese at a loss to themselves of 66 killed, 15 missing, and 259 wounded. Lieutenant Knowland, of No. 1 Commando, won a posthumous Victoria Cross for his part in the fighting.

As soon as Miyazaki heard that Ramree Island had been occupied he feared that the 26th Division might land in his rear, so he ordered the "Matsu" Detachment to break off the engagement and withdraw to the An Pass, which was vital to the 54th Division's communications. By February 18, the 25th Indian Division had relieved the Commando brigade.

Miyazaki had received heavy casualties but had skillfully avoided the destruction of his force.

It will be remembered that during February IV Corps and XXXIII Corps had crossed the Irrawaddy and by March 1 Meiktila had fallen. Also at this time the Chinese were asking for an air lift of their forces in Burma to take part in the offensive to regain the two provinces that they had lost a few months previously. Transport aircraft, therefore, were at a premium and S.E.A.C. decided that air supply to XV Corps must cease.

Lieutenant-General Sir Oliver Leese (C.-in-C. A.L.F.S.E.A.) therefore decided to withdraw the 25th and 26th Divisions to India. The 26th Division was withdrawn to prepare for a landing at Rangoon. The Commandos had already been withdrawn to train for a landing on the coast of Malaya.

It is an opportune time to consider the effects of the Arakan campaign. Strangely enough, both sides achieved their main objects. The Japanese, with their depleted forces, prevented XV Corps from breaking into the Irrawaddy valley although this was never XV Corps' intention. On the other hand XV Corps captured Akyab without a shot being fired and Ramree Island with trifling loss, although again the Japanese never had any intention of defending them strongly. Without doubt Miyazaki had done very well against the equivalent of five divisions (25th and 26th Indian, 81st and 82nd West African, and 22nd East African Brigade and 3rd Commando Brigade), supported by overwhelming numbers of aircraft and naval ships. As so often occurred in this campaign, XV Corps' main enemy was geography and the problem of how to apply their superior forces effectively against a skilful enemy in difficult terrain. However, it is now known that Christison had a greater success than he first realised. Only four battalions of both the Japanese 54th and 55th Divisions arrived in time to assist the 33rd Army in its operations against 14th Army. The result was that the 14th Army had nothing but the remains of divisions which had already been virtually destroyed to oppose it in its advance south.

During these operations XV Corps lost 5,089 casualties, of which 1,138 were killed. No. 224 Group (The Earl of Bandon) lost 78 aircraft, but claimed 63 Japanese aircraft destroyed. Fortunately there had never been any serious opposition to the seaborne landings, but during them the Royal Navy fired 23,000 rounds varying from 4-inch to 15-inch calibre. The Navy had landed in all 54,000 men, 800 animals, 11,000 vehicles, and 14,000 tons of stores.

The final seaborne operation of the Burma war was the assault on Rangoon, which started with an airborne attack on Elephant Point, which covered the entrance of the main navigable arm of the Irrawaddy river leading from the sea to Rangoon itself. The amphibious operation for the capture of Rangoon was launched on April 27, while the 14th Army was held up at Prome and the Pegu river.

Two naval forces set sail to give long range protection to the large convoy during its voyage to the mouth of the Rangoon river and to intercept any fleeing Japanese.

The first, under Vice-Admiral Walker, was directed against the Andaman and Nicobar Islands, covering Rangoon from the west. It consisted of the battleships Queen Elizabeth and Richelieu, the cruisers Cumberland, Suffolk, Ceylon, and Tromp, the escort carriers Empress and Shah, six destroyers, and two resupply oil tankers. On the morning of April 30, Walker bombarded targets in the Nicobars and in the evening put in airstrikes and naval bombardments on to airfields, docks, and shipping at Port Blair in the Andamans. Before leaving the area on May 7, Walker also attacked Victoria Point and Mergui near to the Malay border and returned for a second strike at Port Blair and the Nicobars.

The second naval force consisted of three destroyers under Commodore A. L. Poland. On the night of April 29–30 Poland intercepted a convoy of small ships carrying about 1,000 men and stores from Rangoon to Moulmein. He sank ten craft and picked up some survivors.

At 0230 hours on May 1 a visual control post was dropped as a marker for a parachute landing. Thirty-eight Dakotas dropped a composite battalion of the 50th Gurkha Parachute Brigade at 0545 hours. There were five minor casualties. A further 32 casualties were caused amongst the Gurkhas when some Liberators, aiming at another target, dropped a stick of bombs on the paratroopers. The Gurkhas overcame a small force of 37 Japanese holding Elephant Point itself. The way was then clear for landing craft carrying the assault troops to advance up the river as soon as any mines had been swept.

Aircraft flying over Rangoon saw the words "Japs gone" and "Extract Digit" painted on the roof of Rangoon Jail. Wing-Commander A. E. Saunders (commanding No. 110 Squadron R. A. F.), seeing this well known R.A.F. slang and seeing no signs of the enemy, landed at Mingaladon Airfield, but unfortunately damaged his Mosquito in the craters on the runway. Saunders, having contacted the British prisoners-of-war in Rangoon Jail and hearing that the Japanese had evacuated Rangoon on April 29, went down to the docks and sailed down the Rangoon River in a motor launch to report that the Japanese had gone. Meanwhile, the brigades of the 26th Division moved up the Rangoon river in landing craft and soon occupied Rangoon. It was a tragedy that Colonel Dick Ward, who had been Commander Royal Engineers of the 17th Indian Division from its retreat from Moulmein in 1942 to India and had fought throughout the campaign, was killed when the landing craft in which he was travelling in the van to occupy Rangoon on May 2, 1945 struck a mine.

The battles for Mandalay and Meiktila were over. The Japanese 15th Army which had attacked Kohima/Imphal, and the 33rd Army had both suffered a major defeat. The 33rd Army had been severely mauled by the Chinese and Stilwell's N.C.A.C. (including the British 36th Division). During their counter-attack to recapture Meiktila, their losses were again heavy. The 18th Division also had suffered 1,773 casualties, which was about one-third of its strength and lost about half of their 45 guns. The 49th Division, which (being fairly new in Burma) started with a total strength of 10,000, suffered 6,500 casualties and lost all but three of its 48 guns. Casualties amongst the other divisions were of a similar order. As the official British history states of this period, the Burma Area Army had virtually ceased to exist as a fighting force. Already, by August 1944, the Southern Army had been told that it could expect no further reinforcements in men or matériel from Japan, and the divisions were now living on their own fat.

The 28th Army, which was mainly concerned with defending the coast of Burma, had a small force (72nd Independent Mixed Brigade) in the Mount Popa-Chauk-Yenangyaung area but, as related, only four battalions of the 54th and 55th Divisions facing XV Corps were ever deployed in Central Burma to oppose the 14th Army.

General Leese had ordered Slim to reduce the strength of his army to four and two-thirds divisions, which was the maximum number which could be supplied by air during his drive south. XXXIII Corps (Stopford) was to advance down the Irrawaddy valley from Yenanyaung, via Magwe and Allanmyo to the railhead at Prome and on towards Rangoon if it had not already been captured. IV Corps (Messervy) was to use the main road route to Rangoon via Pyabwe, Pyinmana, Toungoo, and Pegu. Each corps would consist of two motorised infantry divisions and one

Oil blaze started by allied Beaufighter attack on pump station, Burma.

armoured brigade.

The plan was that each corps would move in bounds one division at a time passing through the other, from airfield to airfield, supplied by air-landed stores at each point. Travelling with the divisions would be a large number of airfield construction engineers. As the left flank of Messerby's IV Corps would be in the air, Mountbatten decided to organise the loyal Karens in the hills flanking his advance into levies to protect his eastern flank. Over 3,000 of these fine guerrilla fighters were recruited, and Messervy had then no reason to worry about any unexpected attack from that direction as the Karens were only too glad of the chance to kill Japanese.

Japanese officer hands his sword to a Gurkah officer, Burma, Sept 1945.

Each corps had a distance of 350 miles to go to its objective. XXXIII Corps consisted of the 7th and 20th Indian Divisions and the 268th Indian Infantry Brigade, plus the 254th Indian Tank Brigade. IV Corps consisted of the 5th and 17th Indian Divisions and the 255th Indian Tank Brigade. Each corps had its own artillery component which included two medium regiments with XXXIII Corps and one medium regiment with IV Corps. There was a special headquarters Royal Engineer Regiment to control the forward airfield engineers and bridging companies with each corps.

A brigade from the 19th Indian Division accompanied IV Corps and garrisoned its communications as it advanced.

Stopford was held up at Pyabwe by the fine defence of the remnants of the famous 18th Division (now only 2,000 strong) which had captured Singapore, had been one of the first divisions to conquer Burma, and had fought for so long on the northern front against Stilwell.

Otherwise there were no hitches except those caused by geography and the weather. Messervy reached Pyinmana on April 19, Toungoo on the 22nd, and Pegu, within 50 miles of Rangoon, on May 1. At Pegu a Japanese improvised brigade, made up of training unit personnel and numbering 1,700 men, delayed his advance. Unseasonable heavy rain on May 2 stopped IV Corps' advance abruptly. However, the engineers managed to clear 500 mines and to throw a bridge across the Pegu river and at 0930 hours on May 4, IV Corps continued its advance. On May 6 the 1/7th Gurkhas met a column of the Lincolnshire Regiment from the 26th Division, which had advanced northwards from Rangoon.

Meanwhile XXXIII Corps advanced down the Irrawaddy valley. Stopford captured Chauk on April 18 and Magwe and Yenangyaung on April 21, overcoming resistance from the 72nd Independent Mixed Brigade and some battalions from the 28th Army. Allanmyo on the Irrawaddy was captured on April 28 and Stopford entered Prome on May 3. A patrol from XV Corps, advancing from Taungup, contacted him shortly afterwards so that by that date all three corps of Leese's forces were in touch. The Burma victory was now complete.

On June 1, 1945, a 12th Army was formed under command of General Stopford to control mopping-up operations, including the re-establishment of civil government. The 12th Army consisted of IV Corps in the Sittaung valley and the 7th and 20th Indian Divisions and the 268th Brigade in the Irrawaddy valley.

IV Corps consisted of the 5th, 17th, and 19th Indian Divisions, and the 255th Tank Brigade. So with the 7th and 20th Indian Divisions and 268th Brigade, Stopford had five divisions and two brigades under command, with the 26th Division awaiting transport for India. His air support was provided by No. 221 Group R.A.F., but now that the monsoon had broken the R.A.F. was not in a position to give good close support to the troops on the ground. Slim, now promoted General, replaced Leese as Commander Allied Land Forces, South East Asia, and on April 16 took up his command in Kandy, Ceylon.

Stopford's main problem was the Japanese 28th Army which still totalled nearly 30,000 troops.

Sakurai, the army commander, had managed to get the remains of his 54th and 55th Divisions back from the coast and delta over the Irrawaddy and into the Pegu Yomas, a series of jungle-covered hills lying between the Irrawaddy valley on the one hand and the Sittang valley on the other, north of Rangoon. Sakurai's object was to break out and join the remains of the Burma Area Army, which was now regrouping east of the wide flowing and flooded Sittang River. At this time the Sittang was flooded as far north as Shwegyin, a distance of nearly 50 miles upstream from the Gulf of Martaban. Sakurai decided therefore to advance on a wide 100-mile front between Toungoo and Nyaunglebin, just west of Shwegyin.

It would be tedious here to attempt to describe the numerous small operations which occurred as Sakurai's 28th Army attempted to cross the road in dispersal groups during May and August, all the while being hunted by Stopford's Indian battalions, tanks, and armoured cars. These operations were carried out mainly by junior officers, and were very important to them.

However, a brief resum6 of the casualties incurred at that time will indicate the intensity of the fighting and the miserable defeat of the remnants of a once fine army.

On June 28, 1945 the strength of the 28th Army was stated to be 27,764. Three months later, on September 22, the 28th Army's reported strength to the Burma Area Army was as follows: present on duty 7,949; in hospital 1,919; and missing 3,822, some of whom were expected to return.

IV Corps' losses over much the same period were 435 killed, 1,452 wounded, and 42 missing.

Thus in effect ended the war in Burma, where an army of ten Japanese divisions, two Independent Mixed Brigades, and about two Indian National Army divisions were not only defeated, but to all intents and purposes, wiped out as a fighting force.

14th USAF B-25 Mitchell bomb Japanese oil storage tanks att Laichokok.

The Americans began the first phase of the battle for Okinawa on March 18 when carrier-borne planes began pounding Japanese airfields on Kyūshū. On the 19th the Americans switched to the naval bases at Kobe, Kure, and Hiroshima and to Japanese shipping in the Inland Sea. Kamikazes and bombers hit back fiercely, damaging Yorktown, Wasp, and Enterprise and setting Franklin ablaze. Task Force 58 began to withdraw on the afternoon of the 19th, and during the next 48 hours was harried by repeated Japanese air attacks. These, however, were fought off by the American fighter pilots, who ran up impressive scores. The tally of Japanese aircraft destroyed between March 18 and 22 was 528, and 16 surface ships were damaged during the same period, including the super-battleship Yamato. Mitscher's force had amply fulfilled its rôle. When the main landings went in on Okinawa, the Japanese were unable to throw in a serious air counter attack for a week.

Next on the schedule was the seizure of the islands of the Kerama Retto group, a task entrusted to the 77th Division under Major-General Andrew D. Bruce. This was a campaign within a campaign, a faithful miniature of the "island-hopping" programme as a whole. A preliminary reconnaissance and bombardment preceded the actual assault, which was launched on the islands of Aka, Geruma, Hokaji, and Zanami on March 26. Initial progress was so rapid that Bruce decided to take Yakabi Island as well, and it fell with minimal resistance on the first day. The Japanese reacted in familiar fashion on Aka and Zanami, pulling back into the interior after conceding the fight for the beaches. The same thing happened the following day when Tokashiki was attacked, together with Amuro and Kuba. The Keramas were declared secure on the 29th, but the Japanese on Aka and Tokashiki insisted on refusing to surrender until the official capitulation of Japan. The occupation of the Keramas was rounded out with the emplacement of two batteries of 155-mm guns on the coral islands of Keise Shima, a mere 11 miles off the Haguchi beaches. These guns would add to the fire-power of the pre-invasion bombardment, and their emplacement on Keise Shima was a repetition of a trick used with great success during the battle for Kwajalein.

Pre-landing bombardment

While the Keramas were still being cleared, the intricate work of preliminary bombardment and minesweeping in the approaches to Okinawa had already been started by Vice-Admiral William H. Blandy's Task Force 52. The first offshore shelling began on March 25, but the job of clearing the dense minefield which the Japanese had laid off the Hagushi beaches was not completed until the evening of the 29th. Blandy himself called it "probably the largest assault sweep operation ever executed". In the week before the assault the American warships pounded the Japanese defences with over 13,000 shells of calibres ranging from 6-inch to 16-inch, while the carrier planes flew 3,095 sorties, covering targets requested by 10th Army. In the last three days, as the offshore obstacles were cleared, the warships steadily shortened the range and intensified their fire. With the method born of experience and the most detailed planning, an intricate naval ballet manoeuvred 1,300 ships into position for the assault on the morning of April 1.

"Land the landing force"

Admiral Turner's order was signalled to the invasion fleet at 0406 hours on the 1st — four and a half hours before the moment scheduled for hitting the beaches with the first wave. As the long ranks of landing-craft jockeyed into position for the approach, the terrain behind the beaches shuddered and smoked like a volcano under the shellfire of the bombardment force. The boats moved off at 0800 in perfect conditions and the run-in proceeded as easily as a peace-time manoeuvre. As the bombardment lifted and the gunfire shifted inland the first boats began to ground, almost exactly on schedule, just after 0830. To the troops the actual landing came as an almost ludicrous anti-climax. "Where are the Japs?" was the question every man was asking as the cautious advance into the interior began. Meanwhile the landings continued without a hitch. By the evening of April 1 over 60,000 troops had landed on Okinawa and had pegged out a beach-head over eight miles wide and over two miles deep in places.

"An enemy landing attempt on the eastern coast of Okinawa on Sunday morning was completely foiled, with heavy losses to the enemy." That was how the Japanese boasted of the feint attack made by 2nd Marine Division (Major-General Thomas E. Watson) on the far side of the island from the Hagushi beaches. The Marines had made it look like a genuine attempt, with eight waves of boats dressed in line and covered by bombardment. They moved in simultaneously with the approach to the Hagushi

beaches, reversed course precisely at 0830, and headed back to their parent vessels. The same performance was made on the morning of the 2nd and the force was then withdrawn.

Fast progress

On the second and third days the Marines and infantry pushed right across the island and cut it in two, with 96th and 7th Divisions wheeling to the south on the right flank and feeling out the first serious Japanese resistance around Momabaru. By the evening of April 3 interrogated Japanese civilians and liberated P.O.W.s had informed the advancing troops that the main Japanese forces had pulled back to the south. The puzzle of the non-existent enemy had been solved: the battle for Okinawa had still to begin.

The push to the south was carried out by XXIV Corps: 96th and 7th Divisions, who began the cautious probing of Ushijima's defence outposts. For both divisions, April 5 marked the first day when genuine resistance at last was encountered. The advance continued during the next three days but by April 9 both divisions had been fought to a halt and XXIV Corps had not attained its prescribed objective. On the 9th the 383rd Infantry fought its way on to Kakazu Ridge but were forced to withdraw after a bloody fight. A "powerhouse attack" on April 10 was also repulsed, and the Japanese were still very much in possession of their strongpoint at Kakazu on the 12th. The first round had undoubtedly gone to the Japanese in precisely the sort of battle that Ushijima had planned. American morale was also depressed by President Roosevelt's death, which the Japanese promptly

Landing craft unload vehicles and stores, 'Yellow Beach' Okinawa, 13 Apr 1945.

exploited for propaganda. "We must express our deep regret over the death of President Roosevelt," ran one leaflet. "The 'American Tragedy' is now raised here at Okinawa with his death. Not only the late President but anyone else would die in the excess of worry to hear such an annihilative damage. The dreadful loss that led your late leader to death will make you orphans on this island. The Japanese special assault corps will sink your vessels to the last destroyer. You will witness it realised in the near future."

In the overview the Japanese were whistling in the dark: they certainly had little to boast about as far as naval victories were concerned. On April 7 the "Special Sea Attack Force" had sortied on a one-way mission to Okinawa. It was a suicide run, aimed at sending the superbattleship Yamato into the midst of the American invasion fleet and dealing out as much destruction as possible before meeting her inevitable end. But Yamato had been sunk by carrier planes before she had even sighted Okinawa. With the grip of the American navy unshaken, it was the Japanese who remained the "orphans of Okinawa", for all the local successes they might win. Much more important was the nature of the battle itself, with the Japanese having to accept the consequences of their defensive strategy. The cost of halting XXIV Corps by April 12 had been grievous: about 5,570 for the Japanese and 451 for the Americans. Despite this twelve-fold imbalance, 32nd Army now went over to the offensive to try to exploit the discomfiture

Harbour installations taken by plane from USS Franklin CV-13, Naha City, Okinawa, 10 Oct 1944.

of XXIV Corps by pushing it back to the north.

In two days of intense fighting the Japanese counter-attack, carried out by components of 62nd and 24th Divisions, was repelled at all points. It was a costly deviation from the basic strategy of staying in strongpoints and letting the Americans suffer the losses. By dawn on the 14th stalemate had settled once again over the front line.

Meanwhile Buckner had reversed the original plan of tackling southern Okinawa before clearing the north of the island, and had unleashed Geiger's Marines (6th Marine Division) on April 3. Driving north-eastwards along the nar row "neck" of Okinawa, the 6th Marines had reached the sea and cut off the Motobu Peninsula by April S. But it took them another 12 days to clear the peninsula and they had to exert every effort to crush the main Japanese position at Yae-Take with concentric attacks. Not until the 20th was Japanese resistance in the peninsula broken, and enough Japanese escaped to the hills to begin organised guerrilla warfare.

After changing his plan and clearing northern Okinawa, Buckner also decided to press ahead with capturing Ieshima, the 5-mile-long oval island 3½ miles off the Motobu Peninsula. The Japanese had built three airstrips on Ie shima and that was Buckner's main objective: to seize the island and use it as a natural aircraft-carrier to intensify the air umbrella over the Okinawa battlefield. Ie shima was a formidable nut to crack. The 2,000 troops on the island had, by exploiting civilian labour, made it a miniature Iwo Jima as far as prepared defence positions were concerned. Major-General Andrew D.

Bruce's 77th Division was earmarked for the capture of Ie shima, and the landings went in on April 16. Despite vigorous resistance, the 77th Division had overrun the western half of the island with its airstrips by the end of the 16th. But the Japanese still held out in Ie town. Five more gruelling days were needed before the island was declared secure, and even then the fighting continued until the 24th. The fight of Ie shima epitomised the bitterness of the Okinawa campaign; commenting on it, General Bruce said that "the last three days of this fighting were the bitterest I ever witnessed".

Surprise attack

Back on the southern front, Buckner was preparing to succeed with stealth where open attacks had failed: a surprise attack on the Shuri defences, pushing deep into the Japanese lines and bypassing strongpoints such as the Kakazu Ridge. The attack was set for April 19 and was to be launched by a surprise penetration by General Hodge's 27th Division on the 18th. Hodge summed it all up when he said: "It is going to be really tough. There are 65,000 to 70,000 fighting Japs holed up in the south end of the island, and I see no way to get them out except blast them out yard by yard." The attack of April 19 was a complete failure and cost XXI V Corps 720 casualties. The Japanese fought like furies and held off all the American attempts to slip round their strongpoints.

The zones of fire of their artillery and mortars had been carefully drawn and covered all sectors of the front. One regimental commander in the 96th Division commented bitterly after the battle: "You cannot bypass a Jap because a Jap does not know when he is bypassed." Despite their failure in the attack of April 19 the Americans had no choice but to keep up the pressure on the Shuri defences. When the fighting died down with the coming of darkness on the 19th a gap of nearly a mile yawned between 27th and 96th Divisions and General Griner, commander of the 27th, knew that it must be plugged. But the attack of April 20 went the same way as that of the 19th. This time the problem was a Japanese strongpoint which squarely blocked the line of advance west of Gusukuma towards the Machinato airfield — a strongpoint which had got the very best out of the terrain, was heavily manned, and which had to be cleared out, not bypassed. The Americans called it "Item Pocket" and it took them another exhausting week before it fell. Impromptu names for the key landmarks — "Charlie Ridge", "Brewer's Hill", "Dead Horse Gulch" — became feared and hated names during the incessant fighting between April 20 and April 27, when the Pocket was eventually declared secure. Weeks later, however, Japanese were still emerging from the deep bolt-holes and caves which had given the position its strength.

In the meantime the 7th, 27th, and 96th Divisions battered away at the outer Shuri defences on the centre and left of the front. On the latter sector the Japanese had based their defence on "Skyline Ridge", blocking the approach to Unaha and Yonabaru airfield. In the centre, Kakazu Ridge was still in Japanese hands.

While the fight for Item Pocket raged on the right flank, the Americans struggled painfully forward until at last, by April 24, they had taken both Kakazu and Skyline Ridges. After three weeks' ordeal the outer shell of the Shuri defences had finally been cracked.

At the end of April, Buckner reshuffled his front-line divisions, many units of which were badly in need of a rest. The 27th Division was relieved by the 1st Marine Division on April 30, and the 6th Marine also earmarked for a shift south to the front. The fall of Item Pocket on April 27 was followed by an exact replica of the preceding seven days — and then, on May 4, the Japanese unleashed a counter-offensive aimed at smashing the centre of 10th Army and driving its fragments into the sea. It was an ambitious plan, envisaging amphibious landings deep in the rear of the American positions — but it suffered the same fate as the earlier Japanese attack. The amphibious operation was a total fiasco. Despite a temporary breakthrough in the centre and the recapture of Tanabaru Ridge, the Japanese 24th Division had shot its bolt by the 7th and Ushijima had no choice but to fall back on the defensive, having achieved little but to delay the American advance for just under a week. (During the fighting for the Tanabaru Ridge the news of the German surrender reached Okinawa. "Well, now," said a colonel of the 17th Infantry Division, as he sniped at the Japanese with an M1 carbine, "if we just had the Japs off the escarpment we'd be all right, wouldn't we?")

Once Ushijima's counter-attack had been safely held, Buckner saw in it a chance for a breakthrough. The attack had drawn the last fresh Japanese reserves into the line, and a prompt resumption of the initiative could well prove decisive. The result was the renewal of the attack on May 10 and its culmination on the 21st with the clearing of a "funnel" on the left flank which enabled the 7th Division to edge forwards into the inner ring of the Shuri defences. In this phase the decisive actions were the clearing of the eastern sides of Conical and Sugar Hills, which bent back the extreme right wing of the Japanese line. Plotted on a map, it seemed that the way was open for the rolling-up of the front from the east — but the Japanese remained in firm control of their positions and no breakthrough came. And now, in the fourth week of May, the elements sided with the Japanese. The rain poured down and the battlefield of Okinawa dissolved in mud.

Transport was paralysed and it was impossible to move heavy equipment through the floods and quagmires-but there was no diminution of the pressure. With the Japanese centre north of Shuri still rock steady, Buckner ordered the flanking divisions to intensify operations and bend back the Japanese wings as far as possible. It was an exhausting and undramatic process. With every day's new advances the "bulge" being formed round Shuri seemed to herald the total envelopment of Ushijima's men — but still the Japanese refused to break and the casualties continued to soar. With the rain and the mud and the pattern of attrition in men's lives (one dead American for every ten dead Japanese by the end of May) the battle of Okinawa was taking on the nature of the most hideous trench-warfare pounding match of World War I — and with as few obvious results.

Yet now at last the persistence of the Americans was rewarded.

Japanese POWs march towards a dock to embark on a ship to Hawaii, 27 June 1945.

Even before the ominous constriction of the flanks of the 32nd Army in the last weeks of May, General Ushijima had made the decision to yield the Shuri Line and withdraw to the south after a conference with his staff on May 21. The consensus of opinion had been that to hold on at Shuri would only mean that the 32nd Army would be destroyed earlier than necessary, without having inflicted sufficient losses on the Americans. The 32nd Army would make its last stand at the southern tip of Okinawa. Supplies and wounded began moving south on the night of May 22–23, heading for the positions previously constructed by the 24th Division.

The Japanese retreat

With the rearguard holding on in front of Shuri, the Japanese pulled out with skill and discipline, and their move was largely completed by the end of May. The Japanese move was helped by the sluicing rains and the lowering overcast, which seriously impeded American aerial reconnaissance. From May 26, however, the long Japanese columns were kept under general surveillance from the air: and a 10th Army staff meeting on the evening of May 30 reached the conclusion that although the Japanese were still holding before Shuri, their line was little but a tough shell. It was widely believed that Ushijima had made his decision too late and that the campaign was all over bar the mopping-up. Once again it was a serious under-estimation of the actual situation.

Japanese Navy destroyer is attacked by US B-25 Mitchell.

Shuri fell at long last on May 31, but Buckner's divisions did not, as expected, trap the 32nd Army in a pocket and wipe it out. Nor were they able to prevent it from pulling back and forming yet another solid front in the south. For this the Americans could certainly blame the adverse weather conditions: "We had awfully tough luck to get the bad weather at the identical time that things broke," lamented Buckner.

Thus the scene was set for the last round of the battle for Okinawa. The southern end of the island is best described as a downward-pointing arrowhead. The Shuri Line had crossed the shank of the arrowhead above the barbs; and now the 32nd Army had pulled right down into the very tip of the arrow.

An amphibious operation coped with the western barb of the arrowhead, the Orotu Peninsula, trapping the remnants of Rear-Admiral Minoru Ota's naval troops and wiping them out by June 15 after a ten-day battle. Meanwhile the first attacks on the main Japanese position behind the Yaeju-Dake Ridge had begun.

It took five murderous days-June 12–17-to crack the Yaeju-Dake position: five days in which the fighting was as intense as ever. The Japanese still had to be blasted and burned from their foxholes, and a new American flame-throwing tactic was to bring up a 200-foot fuel supply hose from which to spray napalm on Japanese positions. By June 17 the survivors of the 32nd Army had been blasted out of their front-line position and compressed into an area eight miles square. After more than two and a half months of superb endurance, the men of the 32nd Army had reached the end of their tether. Between the 18th and the 21st they were split into three independent pockets and it was obvious that the end was near. Buckner sent a personal appeal to Ushijima to see reason and save the lives of his last men. Ushijima received it with vast amusement. He radioed his last message to Tokyo on the evening of the 21st, and he and his chief-of-staff, General Isamu Ota, committed ritual hara-kiri the same night. The last organised resistance — on Hill 85, between Medeera and Makabe — was broken on the 21st. Although "Old Glory" was formally raised over Okinawa at the 10th Army headquarters on the morning of the 22nd, mopping-up operations lasted until the end of the month; and the Ryûkyizs campaign was officially declared ended on July 2.

The cost

The Allies had conquered Okinawa and were now only 350 miles from Ky sh itself. The objective of "Iceberg" had been achieved, but at a terrifying cost. Total American battle casualties were 49,151. The Americans had lost 763 aircraft and 36 ships sunk; another 368 of their ships had been damaged. But the Japanese had lost 110,000 men, including conscripts and drafted civilians, and even this has to be an approximate figure. Only 7,400 Japanese prisoners were taken on Okinawa-most of them in the last days when the 32nd Army was disintegrating. Ten major kamikaze attacks had been thrown against Okinawa, using up some 1,465 aircraft; and the total number of suicide sorties was 1,900. The Japanese losses in aircraft were staggering: 7,800. The Imperial Navy lost 16 ships sunk and four damaged.

What did the Okinawa campaign prove? First and foremost, it gave a bitter foretaste of what the Allies could expect if they ever tried to land on Japanese soil. It was the bloodiest fight of the Pacific war. But above all it proved that nothing could stop the Allies in the Pacific from moving where they wanted, even if it did mean killing every Japanese in their way. And Ushijima himself paid tribute to this in his last message to Tokyo. "Our strategy, tactics, and technics all were used to the utmost and we fought valiantly," he reported. "But it was as nothing before the material strength of the enemy."

Kamikaze mentality

The ambitious "SHO" plan which had thrown the massed strength of the Combined Fleet against the Americans at Leyte had been motivated by the kamikaze mentality: to do as much damage as possible with inferior resources. And the same held true of one of the most bizarre episodes in naval history: the suicide sortie of the Yamato during the opening phase of the long battle for Okinawa, in April 1945.

Japan's defensive strategy was based on the idea of "Dunkirking" the spear head troops, once they had got ashore, and disrupting the Allied offensive plan by raising as much havoc as possible. And it was to this end that the "Special Sea Attack Force" was formed. It consisted of the Yamato and a light destroyer escort. Using literally the last dregs of the country's fuel oil stocks, the Yamato would make straight for the invasion beaches at Okinawa, deal out maximum destruction to the

Call to surrender from LCI along southern beaches, Okinawa.

American invasion fleet, then beach herself and fight to the last shell available for her huge 18-inch guns.

Under the command of Vice-Admiral Seiichi Ito, the force sailed from Tokuyama in Japan's Inland Sea on the afternoon of April 6: Yamato, surrounded by a ring of eight destroyers and the light cruiser Yahagi. The Japanese squadron had barely cleared Japanese territorial waters before it was spotted by American submarines patrolling the Bungo Strait, between the islands of Shikoku and Ky sh . Once out at sea, Ito altered course to the west, steering into the East China Sea preparatory to a last turn to the south for the final run down to Okinawa, and his ships were sighted at 0822 hours on the 7th by reconnaissance aircraft from Admiral Marc Mitscher's Task Force 58. A mighty strike of 380 dive-bombers and torpedo-bombers took off from Mitscher's carriers at 1000, when the Japanese force was some 250 miles away — just before Yamato and her frail ring of escorts swung to the south. Around noon the first contact was made and the final ordeal of the Yamato began.

The American pilots were impressed by the massive A.A. fire which came up at them: the Japanese had learned the lesson of air power well, and by the time of her last voyage Yamato bristled with no less than 146 25-mm A.A. guns. Most impressive of all, however, were the San-Shiki shells fired by her main armament, which may be best described as 18-inch shotgun shells. Yamato's main battery was designed for use in the antiaircraft rôle and the San-Shiki shells were crammed with incendiary bullets. The idea was that the shells would be fired into a group of enemy aircraft; the shells would then burst, like a shotgun fired into a flock of birds, mowing down the enemy planes. It was found, however, that the terrifying blast of Yamato's 18-inch guns when fired at maximum elevation only served to disrupt the main volume of A.A. fire. The San-Shiki shells proved to be a failure, like so many other impressive-sounding Japanese ideas. The Japanese had the weather — squalls and low clouds — on their side, but little else. The Special Attack Force had no fighter cover whatever and the American bombers were able to make almost unimpeded progress as repeated waves swept in to the attack. The ring of Japanese destroyers soon broke up under the stress of constant manoeuvre to avoid torpedoes. Pounded to a wreck, Yahagi sank shortly after 1400 hours; and 25 minutes later came the turn of Yamato. She had taken a fearful beating; at least ten torpedoes had hit her, plus seven bombs. Her crew was unable to cope with the inrush of water, or keep her upright by counterflooding. Yamato finally capsized and sank at 1425. Admiral Ito and nearly all the ship's company of 2,400 men went down with her. Four of the escorting destroyers were sunk as well, and the battered survivors turned for home.

An era ends

Such was the Battle of the East China Sea on April 7, 1945. It was the end of the Dreadnought age — the last time that a battleship was sunk by enemy action on the high seas. The wheel had indeed come full circle since Pearl Harbor in December 1941, when the superb Japanese carrier arm had proved the vulnerability of the battleship once and for all. Yamato's sacrifice was totally useless; she had never even sighted Okinawa, let alone taken any pressure off the gallant Japanese garrison there. On the Japanese side of the ledger there was only one completely insignificant flicker of success: a kamikaze hit on the carrier Hancock.

The remnants

Cowering in the Japanese home ports lay the remnants of the Imperial Navy. At Yokosuka there was the battleship Nagato, in her heyday the strongest battleship in the world with her 16-inch main armament. Her last action had been Leyte Gulf, where she had escaped the holocaust of the battleships. Now in the summer of 1945 she was inoperable, inglorious, with her funnel and foremast removed to assist camouflage. The rump of the battle

Remains of Japanese suicide troops who attacked airfield at Yontan, Okinawa, 24 May 1945.

fleet lay at Kure, Japan's great naval base. There were the Ise and Hyuga, absurdly converted to seaplane-carriers by the removal of their after turrets. With equal absurdity they had been classified the 4th Carrier Division of the 2nd Fleet in November 1944. In March 1945 they had finally been taken off the active list and now served as A.A. batteries. Also at Kure was the Haruna, the last survivor of the "Kongo" class battle-cruisers built on the eve of World War I. With the Kongos Japanese designers had shown the world that they had seen through the inherent weaknesses of the battle-cruiser concept by specifying their order for fast battleships; and the Kongos had been extensively reconstructed between the wars. Another genuine museum-piece at Kure in 1945 was the old target-ship Settsu, whose construction had helped place Japan fourth after Britain, the United States, and Germany as a Dreadnought naval power.

The Combined Fleet

There were seven Japanese aircraft-carriers in home waters. First among them was the little Hosho, the first carrier in the world to be designed as such from the keel up, which had been launched after World War I. When she served as fleet carrier training ship, most of the Japanese Navy's crack aircrews learned their trade aboard her. She had survived Midway as Yamamoto's last serviceable carrier and was still in service in 1945. The other six carriers — Ibuhi, Amagi, Katsuragi, Kaiyo, Ryuho, and Junyo — represented the losing struggle to restore carrier protection and hitting-power to the Combined Fleet. Apart from destroyers and submarines still in service, the only other major units of the Combined Fleet in Japanese ports in 1945 were six cruisers.

With American carrier planes now able to range at will over the Japanese homeland, it was only a matter of time before these sorry survivors were singled out for destruction. Admiral Halsey planned it personally: it was to be a formal revenge for Pearl Harbor, an all-American operation without the British Pacific Fleet. It took the form of a fearsome three-day blitz on the Japanese naval bases, concentrating on Kure. Between July 24 and 26, 1945, the American carrier forces struck round the clock. In those hectic days they sank the Amagi, Ise and Hyuga, Haruna, Settsu, and five cruisers, effectively destroying Japanese

hopes of forming a possible suicide squadron from their last heavy warships. If any one date is required for the formal annihilation of the Japanese fleet, it may be set as July 24–26, 1945.

Inglorious end

The postwar fate of the Japanese warships which survived Halsey's Blitz of July 1945 was inglorious. Nagato, last of the battle fleet, was used as a target ship during the Bikini Atoll atom test in 1946, together with the cruiser Sakawa. The other cruisers and carriers were either used as targets, scrapped, or sunk at sea by the victors — the Americans in particular sank a hecatomb of surrendered Japanese submarines off Gato Island in April 1946.

The fate of the last vessels of the Imperial Japanese Navy was the grim end to a remarkable story. Japan's emergence as a modern power only dates from the last three decades of the 19th Century. By careful study of the best European models, she built a navy second to none in either matériel or fighting spirit in under 30 years. In that period Japanese naval designers not only participated in the birth of the Dreadnought era: they proved again and again that they could lead the world in laying down new concepts for the development of the fighting ship and the evolution of naval warfare.

What went wrong? It is now generally accepted that Japan's decision to go to war in December 1941 was a calculated risk, a gamble which came within an ace of success. But as far as the total defeat of her prime instrument of war in the Pacific — the Combined Fleet — is concerned, several serious errors stand out. The first is that in 1941 the Combined Fleet was a contradiction

Funeral service Lt Gen Simon Bolivar Buckney Jr, former CG of US 10th Army, killed in action, Okinawa.

in terms. Its carrier force was superb but the battlefleet — the big gun — was still looked to as the weapon which would bring decisive victory. Submarine strategy was totally misguided on the Japanese side, whereas the Americans used their submarines correctly and reaped the rewards. Above all, however, the Japanese naval strategists had to cut their coat according to their cloth: the one thing they could not afford was a war of attrition, and this they got. The Guadalcanal campaign, for example, cost them the equivalent of an entire peace-time fleet-losses which could never be replaced. The very speed with which the Americans assumed the offensive in the Pacific, never to lose it, showed what a narrow margin the Japanese Navy had.

And the result was an unreal metamorphosis which led the Japanese into building huge white elephants like Shinano and the aircraft-carrying "1–4400" submarines. It saw the Combined Fleet change from an instrument of the offensive and of victory to a sacrificial victim whose purpose was only to stave off defeat. This process first became dominant at the time of the Marianas campaign in June 1944, and it was the leitmotif of the final destruction of the Combined Fleet. That there was great heroism among the men who took Yamato out on her last voyage cannot be doubted. But the former cold professionalism which had carried the Japanese Navy to its high tide of victory in the summer of 1942 was gone. In ships, in men, and in men's ideas, too much had been lost in the disastrous naval operations in the Solomon Islands, at Midway, and in the battle of Leyte Gulf.

Damage after B-29 incendiary attack on Tokyo.

The defeat of Germany took precedence over that of Japan, but within the limits that this imposed, the overall Allied strategy with regard to Japan was to advance by way of the central and southwest Pacific to recapture the Philippines or Formosa with the objective of eventually blockading and possibly invading Japan herself.

When American forces captured the Marianas in June 1944, they breached Japan's inner defence perimeter and brought the Japanese home-land within striking distance of long-range bomber aircraft. At this time too, the greater part of Japan's naval air arm was destroyed in the Battle of the Philippine Sea.

On October 3, 1944, the American Chiefs-of-Staff decided on the strategy to be adopted for the remainder of 1944 and for the following year. MacArthur was ordered to invade Luzon, and Nimitz was to capture one island in the Bonins and one in the Ryūkyūs, the latter for development into an advanced naval and air base for the invasion of Japan contemplated for the autumn of 1945.

Germany surrendered at the beginning of May 1945, and the American Chiefs-of-Staff turned their attention to ending the war against Japan as quickly as possible. With the end of resistance on Okinawa in June 1945, the American forces were in an even better position to blockade Japan, thus cutting her off from the Asian mainland, and to step up their bombing of Japanese cities and so bring the economic life of Japan to a halt. They were also in a good position to invade Japan if this was considered necessary.

General Curtis LeMay, of the 21st Bomber Command, thought that the war could be ended without invading Japan. He was convinced that with an adequate supply of aircraft and bombs, air power on its own could bring about the Japanese surrender. His own command was due to be enlarged by reinforcements from Europe and India, and he therefore saw no difficulty in stepping up the weight of his offensive after April 1945. LeMay based his assumptions on the results of the five incendiary attacks on Japan in March 1945, and his programme for the defeat of Japan comprised attacks on aircraft factories, industrial cities, oil refineries, storage plants, and in addition, minelaying to prevent the import to Japan of food and raw materials from Manchuria, Korea, and China.

The American Joint Chiefs, however, did not think that unconditional surrender could be obtained without a successful invasion of Japan. They saw the close sea blockade of Japan and the intensive bombing offensives from Okinawa, Iwo Jima, and the Marianas as preliminaries to the invasion attempt itself. By these means, Japan's industry and communications, and her people's will to resist, would all be considerably weakened.

On April 3, 1945, the Joint Chiefs instructed General Douglas MacArthur (who would lead the invasion) to begin drawing up the plans for the invasion of southern Kyūshū in November 1945 to secure forward sea and air bases for the main invasion. This was to take place on the Tokyo plain of Honshū in March 1946.

In readiness for the invasion, the command structure in the Pacific was reorganised. MacArthur was given command of all Army forces and resources, while Admiral Nimitz was to be naval commander. On July 10, a third command, the U.S. Army Strategic Air Force for the Pacific, under General Spaatz, was established to control the air forces involved in the invasion. There was to be no supreme commander in the Pacific, and much was to depend on the ability of MacArthur, Nimitz, and Spaatz to cooperate closely together.

MacArthur's and Nimitz's staffs worked on the plans, and on May 25, MacArthur and Nimitz were officially ordered to undertake the invasion of Kyūshū (Operation "Olympic") on November 1, 1945, and of Honshū (Operation "Coronet") on March 1, 1946. When the Japanese capitulated in August 1945, planning for the invasion had reached an advanced stage.

Prior to the invasion, the Strategic Air Force, based on the Marianas and on Okinawa, would continue its offensive against Japanese industrial centres and lines of communication. To aid this programme, Okinawa and Ie Shima were to be developed into a massive air base for some 240 squadrons.

Meanwhile, the Fast Carrier Force would make repeated attacks to destroy Japanese naval and air forces and disrupt land and sea communications.

The Far East Air Force was to neutralise the Japanese air forces in Japan itself and stationed on the Asiatic mainland, harass shipping routes between Asia and Japan, and destroy communications on Kyūshū along with defence installations there.

Operation "Olympic"

Operation "Olympic" had to be under taken with troops at

hand. The bulk of the forces for the invasion of Japan were to be American, although three divisions from the Commonwealth — one from Britain, one from Canada, and one from Australia — were earmarked for later in the Honsh campaign. A small number of Commonwealth air squadrons would participate, in addition to the British Pacific Fleet.

The U.S. 6th Army, comprising some 500,000 men and commanded by General Walter Krueger, was chosen for the initial assault.

Before the actual invasion, a preliminary operation was to be carried out to occupy the islands lying to the west and south of Ky sh , so that air raid warning facilities, advanced naval anchorages, and sea-plane bases could be established before the landings on Ky sh .

Three corps, each comprising three divisions, were to land on southern Ky sh and establish bridgeheads. I Corps would land in the Miya-zaki area, XI Corps in Ariake wan (bay), and V Amphibious Corps in the bay to the south of Kushikino. Air attacks were planned to prevent the Japanese bringing up reinforcements to the battle area from the north by road or along the coasts. Within the bridgeheads, work was to begin straightaway on the construction of airfields and bases. Following this, additional areas were to be seized for airfields.

The prime objective of Operation "Olympic" was Kagoshima wan, a 50-mile bay which was to be opened up to Allied shipping and through which would flow most of the men and supplies for the Honsh invasion build-up. Kagoshima wan was also to serve as the navy's advance base.

No advance beyond this would be made, the object of "Olympic" being to secure bases for Operation "Coronet".

If the 14 divisions allotted to the 6th U.S. Army were unable to capture and hold southern Ky sh , they could be reinforced from December by three divisions per month, intended for Honsh .

The Navy's task in Operation "Olympic" would be to bring reinforcements and supplies to the 6th Army, to cover and support land operations in Ky sh , to establish a forward base at Kagoshima wan, and to hold island positions necessary for the security of lines of communication.

For Operation "Olympic", Admiral Nimitz divided the American fleet into two — the 3rd and the 5th fleets. The 3rd Fleet, under Admiral William F. Halsey, consisted of a number of fast carrier groups plus supporting battleships, cruisers, and destroyers. Its two main components were Vice-Admiral John Towers's 2nd Carrier Task Force (T.F. 38) and Vice-Admiral H. Bernard Rawlings's British Carrier Task Force (T.F. 37). The 3rd Fleet was to operate against the Kuriles, Hokkaido, and Honsh .

The 5th Fleet, commanded by Admiral Raymond A. Spruance, contained 2,902 vessels, and its main components were the 1st Fast Carrier Force under Vice-Admiral F. C. Sherman (T.F. 58), the Amphibious Force under Admiral Richmond Kelly Turner (T.F. 40), which would land the troops, the Gunfire and Covering Force (T.F. 54) for bombardment and fire support, and T.F. 56, responsible for minesweeping operations. The naval bombardment was to begin eight days before the invasion, and continue until after the launching of the assault.

These were the plans which existed for Operation "Olympic". The second stage of the conquest of the Japanese home islands, Operation "Coronet" — the invasion of Honsh — would have involved even more troops.

Operation "Coronet"

According to the plans that had been drawn up, the troops were to be landed on the Kanto plain, east of Tokyo, a level area with good beaches, which would benefit Allied superiority in armour and mechanisation, and good harbours for the logistic support of the operation. The centre of Japanese political and industrial life was sited, in this region, and the American planners felt certain that a defeat here would firmly convince the Japanese that the war was lost.

Only the general outlines of the plan for Operation "Coronet" were fixed when the Japanese capitulated. The final details had still to be settled. However, it is clear that two American armies under MacArthur's command were to take part — the U.S. 1st Army commanded by General Courtney H. Hodges, and comprising XXIV Corps (Lieutenant-General J. R. Hodge) and III Amphibious Corps (Major-General Roy Geiger); and the U.S. 8th Army under General R. L. Eichelberger, comprising X Corps (Major-General F. C. Sibert), XIV Corps (Major-General Oscar Griswold), and XIII Corps (Major-General Alvan Gillem jnr.).

Air support was expected to come from 40 air groups based on Ky sh , and from a similar force from fields in Iwo Jima, the Marianas, and the Ry ky s.

General Eichelberger's 8th Army was to land in Sagami bay and strike north and east to clear the western shore of Tokyo bay as far north as Yokohama. Armoured forces would simultaneously drive north to cut off any Japanese reinforcements. Some of the armour would then be available to assist the 1st Army in the capture of Tokyo, should this prove necessary. At the same time, other divisions would be used to capture Yokohama.

"KETSU-GO" Plan

In April 1945, Imperial General Headquarters of Japan concluded that American forces, already stationed in the Bonins and the Ry ky s, were quite likely to invade Ky sh with between 15 and 20 divisions in October 1945, and then to invade Honsh in March 1946 with up to 30 divisions. They expected the Americans to intensify incendiary bombing attacks and the close blockade in the summer months, and then to concentrate on the destruction of the Japanese air forces. Consequently they decided it would be expedient to decentralise control.

Imperial General H.Q. formulated a plan for the defence of Japan, namely "KETSU-GO", which divided Japan's home islands, plus Korea, into seven zones. which were all designated certain army areas. The most likely invasion areas, Ky sh (16th Area Army) and Tokyo (12th Area Army) were allotted 65 infantry divisions, two armoured divisions, 25 independent mixed brigades, three guards brigades, and seven tank brigades — in all, well over half the total of forces available. Arrangements were made for one area to reinforce another if necessary, although it was realised that the individual islands might well be isolated from each other. Continuous defences were to be constructed on the probable landing sites, but out of reach of American naval bombardment. It was hoped that coastal defence divisions would contain the invaders in their beach-head, and that mobile assault divisions would then move up and eliminate the enemy.

The plan emphasised the need for the government, the people, and the armed forces to be completely united and for the entire nation to be armed and ready to fight for the homeland. Where few regular troops were stationed, guerrilla forces were to be organised and trained.

On April 8, 1945, Air General Army Headquarters were established under General M. Kawabe, to control air defences. Its tasks were to attempt to hamper the Americans' invasion preparations, to counter American air attacks on Japan, Korea, and the China coast, and also to build up the strength of the air force to counter losses already sustained.

General Kawabe formed a number of special kamikaze units, as he felt these would be the most effective arm against the invaders. These units were dispersed to secret air bases throughout Japan. Obsolete aircraft were converted to kamikaze craft. By the end of June, Kawabe hoped to have 2,000 kamikazes, and a further 1,000 by August.

To meet the invasion, it was estimated that, by August, Air General Army would have 800 fighter and bomber aircraft in addition to the kamikazes, and approximately 13 million gallons of fuel.

With regard to the navy, there were merely 19 destroyers (with only 3,500 tons of fuel for each one) and 38 submarines to repel the invasion. The destroyers were to be kept in the Inland Sea and used within 180 miles of Ky sh and Shikoku, and the largest of the submarines were to attack the American advanced naval bases at Ulithi, Leyte, and Okinawa. Medium-sized submarines were to attack convoys on supply routes to the north while the small submarine craft patrolled home waters.

There was also a secondary fleet which, by July 1945, consisted of 3,294 vessels of various types including suicide boats, midget submarines, and human torpedoes. This fleet was organised into eight squadrons, and in deploying these, priority was given firstly to Ky sh , secondly to the Shikoku coastal area, and finally to the Tokyo coastal area.

The naval air forces had the task of crushing any invasion force whilst it was still at sea. By August 1, 1946, it was estimated that the naval air arm would have approximately 5,145 aircraft. But there would be only two million gallons of fuel for them. Agreements defining the Army and Navy areas of responsibility were drawn up in April, but the proposals were never enacted.

On June 6, 1945, the Chiefs of the Armed Services laid before Japan's Supreme Council a memorandum entitled The Fundamental Policy to be followed henceforth in the Conduct of the War, calling for mass mobilisation. To support their proposed policy, they also submitted two subsidiary papers, Estimates of the World Situation and The Present State of National Power, and these gave no grounds for confidence that the fundamental policy outlined would succeed. The information in the memoranda indicated that Japan would probably not be able to continue the struggle beyond the autumn.

As the Japanese correctly guessed American intentions, so U.S.

Intelligence officers deduced Japanese strategy, and American plans henceforth contained elaborate provisions to counter kamikaze air attacks which could theoretically wipe out the invasion convoys. At Okinawa, overhead fighters had shot down some 60 per cent of attacking kamikazes, and antiaircraft fire accounted for a further 20 per cent. The remaining kamikazes, however, had wrought considerable havoc. It was therefore planned that, commencing eight days before the preliminary phase of Operation "Olympic", American aircraft were to locate and attack concealed kamikaze bases. Bombing of all known kamikaze airstrips within 300 miles of the assault area was to take place in the hope of reducing the kamikaze threat by about one-fifth. B-24 and B-32 aircraft were to patrol selected areas containing known Japanese bases, so that early warning could be given of any impending kamikaze attack, and so that some aircraft could be destroyed on the ground. Close fighter cover would be provided for convoys to ward off kamikazes. Submarines were to give notice of attacks from Korean bases. By these means then, and by the antiaircraft fire from the ships themselves, it was hoped to reduce the damage done by kamikazes. In any case, as they were a wasting asset, the intensity of the attacks was expected to drop as the operation continued. And although the short distances the kamikazes would have to fly would make them difficult to intercept, the disruption of communications and the failure of the Japanese to establish a combined air headquarters would be factors working against their success. Also, at this point, the kamikaze pilots were no longer all volunteers, the available planes were not as suitable as earlier kamakaze craft, and fuel was in short supply.

As for the water-borne suicide craft, these had not proved highly effective at Okinawa, and with regard to the invasion of Japan, the "Olympic" plan included heavy attacks on their potential bases.

And finally, the raising of the divisions to meet the invasion exhausted all Japan's manpower reserves. Many soldiers expected to fight and resist the invaders were poorly trained and badly equipped. In fact the Japanese encountered such difficulty in providing the Kyūshū defenders with adequate weapons that their ability to resist a landing was imperilled. There was also a serious shortage of experienced officers, and most of the technical units were without experienced tradesmen. There were only enough reserve supplies for a limited period, and both fighting formations and lines of communication were short of transport; much of what was available was animal-drawn. Fuel was in extremely short supply.

In comparison, the U.S. 6th Army comprised fully-equipped and experienced veteran formations. The Allied air forces had air supremacy over Japan and would have had no difficulty in disrupting Japanese communications, and any attempts to move reserves.

However, the Americans realised that the invasion of Kyūshū would quite likely result in such a resurgence of national spirit that the Japanese would be fanatical in their fight to the death to defend every inch of ground, as they had done at Okinawa.

The Potsdam Declaration

On July 17, Stalin met with Truman and Churchill at Potsdam. He informed the Western leaders that the Japanese had approached him about peace talks, but seemed unprepared to accept the Allies' demand for unconditional surrender. Truman and Churchill, along with Chiang Kai-shek, issued the Potsdam Proclamation on July 26, reiterating the demand that surrender be unconditional. Otherwise, the proclamation declared, Japan would face "prompt and utter destruction". It did not state that this destruction would be brought about by a new weapon — the atomic bomb.

The debate in top Japanese diplomatic and military circles now revolved around the meaning of the word "unconditional". Did this mean that the nation must surrender, as well as the armed forces? Did it mean that the Emperor would be deposed and the Imperial institution abolished? The Potsdam Proclamation had been silent on this point. Both the diplomats and the high command were determined to support the Emperor, and the generals knew that their men would never accept any agreement which abolished the Imperial institution. In the words of one high-ranking officer, "it would be useless for the people to survive the war if the structure of the State itself were to be destroyed…. even if the whole Japanese race were all but wiped out, its determination to preserve the national policy would be forever recorded in the annals of history, but a people who sacrificed will upon the altar of physical existence could never rise again as a nation."

Col. Paul W. Tibbets, Jr., pilot of the ENOLA GAY, the plane that dropped the atomic bomb on Hiroshima, waves from his cockpit before the takeoff

Hiroshima

One hope for enforcing a Japanese surrender, short of invasion, which was discussed at the White House on June 18, 1945, was a prediction of the highly secret U.S. Army Manhattan Engineer District project that two atomic bombs would be available for operational employment by the end of July. The United States Army Air Forces had already provided everything required to drop the atomic bombs when they were ready. The 509th

Composite Group had been activated in December 1944 under the command of Colonel Paul W. Tibbets, Jr., and included the 393rd Bombardment Squadron with the most advanced model long-range B-29 bombers - the only American aircraft big enough to carry the first atomic weapons.

On August 6, 1945 at 0245 hours the Enola Gay B-29 bomber lifted off from North Field on Tinian Island. At 0815 hours the atomic bomb called "Little Boy" exploded 2,000 feet above the city of Hiroshima, Japan's seventh largest city. Approximately 60,000 out of 90,000 buildings were destroyed or badly damaged. There were an estimated 139,402 casualties, including 71,379 known dead and missing. Among these, were 20,000 school children.

On August 9, a second mission took off bound for Nagasaki with a plutonium bomb called "Fat Man", which exploded 1,750 feet over Nagasaki's industrial sector. Casualties were estimated at 35,000 dead.

In the midst of this debate, on August 6, the first atomic bomb was dropped on Hiroshima. Three days later a second atomic bomb devastated Nagasaki, and the Soviet Union finally declared war on Japan. A conference of the Emperor and his civilian and military advisers was hastily summoned, and met in an air-raid shelter in the grounds of the Imperial Palace in Tokyo shortly before midnight. In the light of the events of the past three days, even the military authorities agreed now that a surrender was unavoidable. Unlike Foreign Minister Togo, however, who advised surrender on the single condition that the Emperor's rights be preserved, the military leaders asked for three other reservations.

First, they wanted to avoid an Allied military occupation of Japan. Second, they wanted to try war criminals themselves. Third, they wanted to disarm their own troops rather than surrender directly to the Allies. War Minister Anami explained that this last proviso could be taken to mean that the Japanese armed forces were not actually defeated, but had decided to stop fighting voluntarily in order to preserve the Japanese land and people from further destruction. When the two sides had expressed their views, the conference was found to be deadlocked. Then the unprecedented happened. The Emperor's advisers actually asked him for his own opinion. Instead of acting according to his advisers' instructions, the Emperor was being asked to advise them. He was to shed the rôle of observer and puppet and make his own decision. Hirohito had already made up his mind, and he soon made it clear that he believed the Foreign Minister's proposal — with only the Emperor's position safeguarded — was more likely to lead to a quick peace settlement and should therefore be accepted. The conference unanimously endorsed the Emperor's decision, and cables were sent within a few hours announcing the Japanese terms.

Later that same day, a reply was received from U.S. Secretary of State James Byrnes. This note explained that the Allies would not accept anything but an unconditional surrender, and that this meant that the Emperor would be subject to the Supreme Commander for the Allied powers. This statement produced another argument in the Japanese cabinet — what did "subject to" mean? At another meeting on the morning of August 14, it was pointed out that Byrnes' note indicated that the Imperial

The mushroom cloud created by the detenation of the atomic bomb over Hiroshima.

institution would not be abolished, and in any case the Japanese Emperors had often been "subject to" the power of the shoguns. Once again, Hirohito was asked for his own opinion, and once again he called for immediate acceptance of the Allied demand. The cabinet acceded to the Imperial will, and it was announced over the radio that Japan had surrendered.

On August 30, the first American occupation forces (including a small British contingent) landed at Yokosuka. Three days later, at nine o'clock in the morning, Japan's new Foreign Minister, Mamoru Shigemitsu, boarded the Missouri in Tokyo Bay. On behalf of the Emperor and the Japanese Government, he signed the official surrender document. General Douglas MacArthur accepted the surrender, a scratchy record of The Star Spangled Banner was played on the ship's speakers, and World War II was over.

Atomic cloud spreading over Nagasaki.

Japanese officers being escorted from the municipal building following the Japanese surrender.

CHRONOLOGY OF WORLD WAR II

	1938
March 11	Anschluss — German annexation of Austria.
September 29	Munich Agreement signed.
October 5	Germany occupies Sudetenland.

	1939
March 14	Slovakia declares its independence.
March 31	Britain and France give guarantee to Poland.
April 7	Italy invades Albania.
May 22	Germany and Italy sign Pact of Steel.
August 23	Molotov-Ribbentrop pact signed between Germany and the Soviet Union.
September 1	Germany invades Poland.
September 1	Britain and France declare war on Germany.
September 17	Soviet Union invades Poland.
November 30	Soviet Union at war with Finland.

	1940
March 12	War between Soviet Union and Finland ends.
April 9	Germany invades Norway and Denmark.
April 14	Allied troops land in Norway.
May 10	Fall Gelb, the offensive in the West, is launched by Germany.
May 10	Churchill becomes Prime Minister of Great Britain.
May 14	Dutch Army surrenders.
May 26	Beginning of evacuation of Dunkirk.
May 28	Belgium surrenders.
June 2	Allies withdraw from Norway.
June 4	Dunkirk evacuation complete.
June 10	Italy declares war on Britain and France.
June 14	Germans enter Paris.
June 21	Italy launches offensive against France.
June 22	France and Germany sign armistice.
June 24	France and Italy sign armistice.
July 3	Royal Navy attacks French fleet at Mers el Kebir.
July 10	Beginning of the Battle of Britain.
September 17	Operation Sealion (the invasion of England) postponed by Hitler.
September 21	Italy and Germany sign Tripartite Pact.
September 27	Japan signs Tripartite Pact.
November 20	Hungary signs Tripartite Pact.
November 22	Romania signs Tripartite Pact.
November 23	Slovakia signs Tripartite Pact.

	1941
January 19	British launch East African campaign offensive.
January 22	Australian troops take Tobruk.
February 6	British capture Benghazi.
February 11	Rommel arrives in Libya.

March 25	Yugoslavia signs Tripartite Pact.
March 27	Yugoslavia leaves Tripartite Pact after coup d'etat.
March 28	Successful British naval action against Italians off Cape Matapan.
April 6–8	Axis forces invade Yugoslavia and Greece.
April 11	U.S.A. extends its naval neutrality patrols.
April 13	Belgrade falls to Axis forces.
April 14	Yugoslav forces surrender.
April 22	Greek First Army surrenders at Metsovan Pass.
May 16	Italians surrender to British at Amba Alagi.
May 20	Germans land on Crete.
May 24	H.M.S. Hood sunk by Bismarck.
May 27	Bismarck sunk by Royal Navy.
June 1	British withdraw from Crete.
June 2	Germany launches Operation Barbarossa against the Soviet Union.
July 27	Japanese troops invade French Indo-China.
September 19	Germans capture Kiev.
September 28	Three-power Conference in Moscow.
December 6	Britain declares war on Finland, Hungary and Rumania.
December 7	Japanese attack Pearl Harbor.
December 8	U.S.A. and Britain declare war on Japan.
December 8	Japanese invade Malaya and Thailand.
December 11	Germany and Italy declare war on the U.S.A.
December 14	Japanese begin invasion of Burma.
December 25	Japanese take Hong Kong.
1942	
February 15	Japanese troops capture Singapore from British.
February 27	Battle of the Java Sea.
February 28	Japanese invade Java.
March 8	Japanese invade New Guinea.
March 17	General MacArthur appointed to command South-West Pacific.
April 9	U.S. troops surrender in Bataan.
April 16	George Cross awarded to Island of Malta by H.R.H. King George VI.
April 26	Anglo-Soviet Treaty signed.
May 6	Japanese take Corregidor.
May 7	Battle of the Coral Sea.
May 20	British troops withdraw from Burma.
May 26	Rommel's Afrika Korps attack British at Gazala.
May 30	Royal Air Force launches first thousand-bomber raid on Germany.
June 4	Battle of Midway.
June 21	Rommel's Afrika Korps take Tobruk.
July 1	Sevastopol taken by Germans.
July 1	First Battle of El Alamein.
August 7	U.S. troops land on Guadalcanal.
August 11	PEDESTAL convoy arrives in Malta.
August 19	Raid on Dieppe.

August 31	Battle of Alam Halfa.
October 24	Second Battle of El Alamein.
November 8	Operation TORCH landings in North Africa.
November 11	Germans and Italians occupy Vichy France.
November 27	French fleet scuttled at Toulon.
1943	
January 14–24	Allied Conference at Casablanca.
January 23	British troops take Tripoli.
February 2	Germans surrender at Stalingrad.
February 8	Red Army captures Kursk.
February 13	Chindits launch first operation into Burma.
February 19	Battle for the Kasserine Pass.
April 19	First Warsaw rising.
April 19	Bermuda Conference.
May 11–25	TRIDENT conference in Washington.
May 13	Axis forces surrender in North Africa.
May 16	Royal Air Force "Dambuster" raid on Mohne and Eder dams.
May 24	U-boats withdraw from North Atlantic.
July 5	Battle of Kursk.
July 10	Allies land in Sicily.
July 25	Mussolini resigns.
September 3	Allies land on Italian mainland.
September 8	Surrender of Italy announced.
September 9	Allies land at Salerno.
September 10	Germans occupy Rome and Northern Italy.
October 13	Italy declares war on Germany.
November 6	Red Army captures Kiev.
November	First Allied conference in Cairo. 23–26
November 28–December 1	Allied conference in Teheran.
December 3–7	Second Allied conference in Cairo.
December 24	General Eisenhower promoted to supreme commander for OVERLORD, the Normandy landings.
1944	
January 22	Allies land at Anzio.
January 27	Red Army raises Siege of Leningrad.
January 31	U.S. forces land on Marshall Islands.
February 1	Battle for Monte Cassino begins.
March 2	Second Chindit operation into Burma.
May 11	Fourth Battle of Monte Cassino.
June 4	U.S. troops enter Rome.
June 6	Operation OVERLORD — Allied landings in Normandy.
June 19	Battle of the Philippine Sea.
July 1	Breton Woods conference.
July 20	Failed attempt to assassinate Hitler — July Bomb plot.
August 1	Second Warsaw rising.
August 4	Allied troops enter Florence.

August 15	Operation DRAGOON — Allied landings in southern France.
August 25	Germans in Paris surrender.
September 4	British troops capture Antwerp.
September	OCTAGON — Allied conference at Quebec. 12–16
September 17	Operation MARKET GARDEN at Arnhem.
September 21	Dumbarton Oaks conference.
October 14	British enter Athens.
October 23	De Gaulle recognised by Britain and U.S.A. as head of French Provisional Government.
October 24	Battle of Leyte Gulf.
December 16	Germans launch campaign in the Ardennes.
1945	
January 4–13	Japanese Kamikaze planes sink 17 U.S. ships and damage 50 more.
January 14	Red Army advances into East Prussia.
January 17	Red Army takes Warsaw.
January 30–February 3	First ARGONAUT Allied conference at Malta.
February 4–11	Second ARGONAUT Allied conference at Malta.
February 6	Allies clear Colmar pocket.
February 19	U.S. forces land on Iwo Jima.
February 26	U.S. 9th Army reaches Rhine.
March 7	U.S. 3rd Army crosses Rhine at Remagen Bridge.
March 20	British capture Mandalay.
March 30	Red Army enters Austria.
April 1	U.S. First and Ninth Armies encircle the Ruhr.
April 1	U.S. forces land on Okinawa.
April 12	President Roosevelt dies and Truman becomes president.
April 13	Red Army takes Vienna.
April 25	U.S. and Soviet forces meet at Torgau.
April 28	Mussolini shot by partisans.
April 29	Germans sign surrender terms for troops in Italy.
April 30	Hitler commits suicide.
May 2	Red Army takes Berlin.
May 3	British enter Rangoon.
May 4	German forces in the Netherlands, northern Germany and Denmark surrender to General Montgomery on Luneburg Heath.
May 5	Germans in Norway surrender.
May 7	General Alfred Jodl signs unconditional surrender of Germany at Reims, to take effect on May 9.
May 8	Victory in Europe Day.
May 10	Red Army takes Prague.
July 17–August 2	Allied TERMINAL conference held in Potsdam.
July 26	Winston Churchill resigns after being defeated in the general election. Clement Attlee becomes Prime Minister of Great Britain.
August 6	Atomic bomb dropped on Hiroshima.
August 8	Soviet Union declares war on Japan.
August 9	Atomic bomb dropped on Nagasaki.
August 14	Unconditional surrender of Japanese forces announced by Emperor Hirohito.
August 15	Victory in Japan Day.
September 2	Japanese sign surrender aboard U.S.S. Missouri in Tokyo Bay.